THE
TIME
OF
THE
FURNACES

Also by Earl Anthony

Picking Up the Gun

THE
TIME
OF
THE
FURNACES

A Case Study of Black Student Revolt

EARL ANTHONY

The Dial Press

New York 1971

To the San Fernando Valley State 19

CONTENTS

It is the time of the furnaces,
And it is only necessary to see the glow.

—José Martí

ONE

A Little
History

In February 1960, David Richmond and three other freshmen from North Carolina Agricultural Technical College sat down at a lunch counter at a Woolworth's five and dime store in Greensboro, North Carolina. The store was similar to most others in the Woolworth chain, except for the fact that it followed the written and unwritten laws of the South and kept blacks and whites segregated in its public facilities and accomodations. And the four A & T students were black. They sat at the counter for one hour until the store closed for the day. They were challenging Southern tradition, the most overt manifestation of America's racism, by asking to be served at a lunch counter along with white customers.

They were refused that day, and the customers and

personnel ignored them; but they were not discouraged, for the refusal was predictable. Yet the consequences of that refusal in Greensboro were not predictable. The four black students went back to their campus and began to organize others to join them in further protests against Woolworth's Southern policy of discriminating against blacks at its lunch counters. This symbolic act by the four black A & T freshmen was the first student demonstration in the civil rights movement to cause national excitement. Within two weeks, sit-ins by black college students had spread to fifteen cities in five southern states.

It was the beginning of the *sit-in movement*. Greensboro '60 was to become an historical signpost, for the sit-in movement was the point at which the non-violent civil rights movement, started by Dr. Martin Luther King and Rosa Parks in '55 in Montgomery, Alabama, gained needed momentum, and it signaled the start of a decade when young black activists, raising the cry for "black power," were to lift black consciousness to its highest level. By exposing the contradictions of racism and economic exploitation inherent in the American system, they brought the country, by the time the '70s came in, to the brink of an irresolvable split between the factions of change and the factions of conservatism.

The sit-in movement was a black student movement, and it paved the way for the black student activism of the '60s. Especially in the South, aware and concerned students began to leave the campuses to organize and participate in sit-ins and other activist forms of non-violent protest.

Historically, students around the world, fired by the

idealism of youth, alienated from vested interests by the very fact that they are tucked away on university campuses, off from the daily grind of life outside their ivy towers, have been a dynamic force for change. The black student movement of the '60s which began in Greensboro was unique among traditional student revolts in that it encompassed more than just a segment of the bourgeoisie-intelligentsia, alienated for a certain period of time—its time in school—and through that alienation developing a new sensitivity to whatever ills are affecting society. The black student movement of the '60s had the added weight of history on its side, for it was composed of blacks who were alienated from the larger world outside the campus long before they entered school—*because of the racism inherent in America.* Therefore the sensitivity developed while they were at college turned them—with their roots deep in that oppressed, exploited class, the American black—into a vanguard for revolution. The black students of the '60s, following the examples of activism initiated by the non-violent movement of the '50s, returned to their "base," the black community, to organize. The focal point was the South, where the contradictions in American society were most blatant and easiest to organize around. The tactic was non-violence.

They worked under the umbrella of a variety of civil rights organizations. Dr. King's SCLC—the Southern Christian Leadership Conference—was one of them. Another was CORE—the Congress of Racial Equality—which organized the first Freedom Rides where black and white activists from all parts of the country rode into the most hostile southern states and were met with violence, terror, and imprisonment. Then there was SNCC—Student Nonviolent Coordinating Committee—an organization consisting of black student activists.

The early '60s was an idealistic time, with many young white students leaving their campuses in the summer to work alongside black students with black people in the South—to assault the monolithic bastion of America's racism. It was the time of the Mississippi Blood Summers, when young white and black students worked and died side by side to register black Mississippians to vote, to organize black political power, and to expose social contradictions by challenging the existing structure on as many levels as possible.

It was the integrationist phase of the black liberation movement, a period extending from Greensboro '60, over many high and low points, to an abrupt end on the Meredith March in the summer of 1966.

On that march came all the civil rights leaders and organizations, walking through Mississippi to appeal to the nation's moral consciousness, for the "thousandth" time, to take a stand against the viciousness and inhumanity of America's racism. One of these organizations was SNCC, whose newly elected chairman, Stokely Carmichael, had come South in '60 to work in the movement and had returned several times while finishing work on a Philosophy degree at Howard University.

SNCC had been known to go further than other organizations in its rhetoric and in its "choice" of what it considered viable alternatives to effect changes that would benefit the black man in America. Its cadres were the black youth—the black students—most of whom by their own admission accepted non-violence only as a tactic, not as a way of life. With many coming from the Black-nationalist-oriented urban North, they had felt the contradictions of having white students organizing in the black communities of the South under the umbrella of a black movement, and had drifted away from the dual doctrines of non-violence and integration.

The position of this dissident faction of the civil rights movement was expounded on the Meredith March by Carmichael, speaking to a rally one hot, humid Mississippi night:

"What do we want?"

The crowd shouted back:

"Black Power!"

Carmichael asked:

"What do we need?"

The crowd shouted back:

"Black Power!"

The black audience that night had been primed by Carmichael and SNCC, and they retorted emphatically with the cry for "Black Power." In the months following the Meredith March this cry swept the nation like a cyclone. It filled the vacuum left by dissatisfaction at the results of non-violent protest in the South, and it appealed to the rising mood of unrest in the urban black communities of the North. The *time* was right for Black Power. Malcolm X, the Harlem Revolt of '64, and Watts '65 had preceded it, and Carmichael and SNCC seized the opportunity and moved rapidly around the country, concentrating on the campuses, pushing the premise that the non-violent and integrationist period of the movement was past.

It was their contention that whites (especially the white youth from the college campuses) should stop organizing in the black communities and turn instead to the white community, where racism had its roots.

The slogan "Black Power," with its strong emotional appeal, did two things instantly. It galvanized black consciousness, giving form and articulation to the new "no more shit" mood of black people; and it elevated a young, dynamic, political-military cadre into the leadership role in the movement for the rights of black people. Soon after this cadre—which in '66 was generally twenty-six years of age and younger—took the reins of leadership, the movement was redefined as the black liberation movement and the objective became human rights, rather than civil rights as sought in the preceding non-violent, integrationist phase.

Consisting almost entirely of black ex-college students, SNCC seized control of the movement in '66 and guided it into the '70s. Among its early tactical decisions designed to serve the loosely framed idealogy of self-determination for black people, one of the most important was that white youth on campuses should go their own way, should "do their thing." Like a rejected, jealous suitor, white youth bridled at this tactical decision at first, but then pulled themselves together. With a psychological boost from SNCC's '67 "Hell No, We Won't Go" stand on black men being drafted into the armed forces, they mounted the partially successful mass peace movement against the Vietnam War. The white college youth could really "get up" for this movement. Not only could they see that the war in Southeast Asia was *not* a matter of halting

Communism, or preserving Democracy, but of Colonialism and Imperialism, they could also see that the *real* choice for them was whether to risk death in the Southeast Asian mud fighting to fatten somebody else's bankroll, or risk jail in the States by fighting for their principles and the right to live.

Following this '66 shift, Stokely Carmichael, the SNCC Chairman and High Priest of Black Power, toured the campuses around the country, as well as the black communities, urging black people to unify and, by collective effort, seize power.

As the spring of '67 came in, black consciousness and rebellion were on a sharp, sudden rise in the black communities and on the black university campuses. Within a few months, blacks were to lay siege to Detroit, Newark, and countless other American cities in the bloodiest period of urban insurrection this country has experienced. *Revolts on black campuses—the source from which the new political-military leadership had sprung—preceded the revolts in the cities.*

At Central State (Ohio), Jackson University, Fisk, and Tennessee State (all black universities), students attempted to apply pressure to make the universities orient their public and private stances to the new black militancy and consciousness. They were met with vocal resistance or complacency from the university administrations themselves, and with savage retaliation from the local and state establishments. Gunfire was exchanged at these campuses. At Texas Southern University, five students, members of the Friends of SNCC, were indicted on the charge of killing a white cop (evidence later showed that the cop was killed by a ricocheting bullet).

In the fall of '66, the black student movement which had begun in Greensboro in '60 reached its pinnacle. Early that fall, attention was focused on San Francisco State College. Here the black student union, led by, among others, Black Panther Party Minister of Education George Murray (the Black Panther Party itself was formed in November '66 by Huey Newton and Bobby Seale while they were students at Merritt Junior College in Oakland, and by other members of that school's Afro-American Student Union) engaged in a new kind of showdown politics with the college administration. Not surprisingly, the administration stance quickly gained the open support of the California State College trustees and Governor Ronald Reagan.

From San Francisco State—where police caused national excitement by garrisoning the campus daily, sometimes in numbers greater than the student population, and often clashing violently with black (and white) student activists—the flames of black student revolt spread. They fanned out eastward to the University of Wisconsin, to CCNY, to Cornell, where black students pulled a tour de force by emerging from their occupation of a campus building fully armed; to the South, where in the spring of '69 three black students at South Carolina State College at Orangeburg were shot to death from behind by state troopers (the Orangeburg massacre received little attention, whereas the killing of four white students at Kent State two years later caused national indignation); and to southern California, at San Fernando Valley State College.

The black campus revolts in '68 were very different from the initial protest in Greensboro in '60. No longer was there an integrationist objective (publicly or privately) among black student activists; the objective of '68 was *separatism*.

It was a logical progression. The black student movement had rejected the myth of integration as the answer for black people in America only after a painful trial and error period of trying to make the myth work ('60 to '66). The successors to these early black student leaders did not repeat their mistakes, and the black student movement, part and parcel of the black liberation movement, became accordingly much more sharply defined by '68 than it had been in '60. *And it was revolutionary in its attitude.*

In '68 an informal national unanimity existed among black student activists on campuses across the country. Racism was accepted as the major problem facing American blacks, and from this it followed that institutional racism, as manifested in the university system (black and white), was a bulwark of America's racist-oriented life style and must be attacked at its roots.

With this emphasis upon racism as the major problem of black people in America, it became unproductive for the black student movement to remain involved with the white student radical movement, which was also in full bloom in '68. Racism was not an issue that consumed every breathing moment of a young white radical's life, however much he was repelled by it on an abstract level. The war in Vietnam was something else again; it was very real to the young white radical student. And so the black student movement and the white radical student movement—SDS, etc.—went their separate ways.

The tactics of the black student activists were determined by their consensus on racism. They attacked it where it affected them—on the university campus, whether at Howard, CCNY, San Fernando Valley, Cornell, or San Francisco State. Their objectives were to make the university more relevant to its black student population, while in turn trying to become more involved with, and therefore relevant to, the larger black community.

The black student activists in '68 closed ranks among themselves in order to become more clearly defined and have the advantage of collective effort. They fought for the following general educational reforms: (1) establishment of an Afro-American Studies program, (2) increased black enrollment (in predominantly white universities), (3) recruitment from the local black community, with more flexible entrance standards, (4) recruitment of a representative percentage of black faculty.

All of these reforms were pressed as demands in the black student revolt at San Fernando Valley State College —a campus located in Los Angeles County in the community of Northridge—on November 4, 1968. And the tactics employed by the students at Valley State were also typical of those used by black students at other white-dominated colleges and universities from '67 to '69. Members of the Black Student Union physically took over the Administration Building, holding the acting president and his staff in the building until they agreed to certain educational reforms that would improve the quality of life for black students on campus.

What distinguished the revolt at Valley State from the other black student revolts of this period was the severity of the penalties imposed on the black students for their activism. Nineteen of them were convicted of felonies in a Superior Court of the state of California, and were sentenced to various prison and probationary terms. These were the first mass felony convictions of student dissidents in the history of the country.

TWO

Archie, Eddie, and Uwezo

When the black student movement was beginning in Greensboro in 1960, Archie Lee Chatman, Jr. was twelve years old and attending John Muir Junior High School in the predominantly black South Central section of Los Angeles. The politics of black liberation were not a part of Archie's world. His concerns at the time were fun and games and schoolwork in the heavily black junior high school, and the schoolwork came easy to him.

Born April 14, 1947, in Los Angeles, California, Archie was the second of three children. There was an older brother John and a younger brother Lewis; there were no sisters. His parents separated when he was three years old, and Archie and his brothers were raised to young manhood singularly by their strong, determined black mother, Ethel Chatman.

Archie started his schooling at Wadsworth Elementary at 47th Street and Central Avenue. Aside from the fact that he came from a religious background, that he went to church regularly and at an early age was imbued with a sense of morality ("I remember when I did something that others thought was bad, which I didn't think I was wrong in doing, I still asked God to forgive me."), there was little in his pre-high school background to distinguish him from his playmates in South Central L.A.

It was when Archie went to high school that he began to encounter experiences that were to shape his views and perspective on himself, experiences that would make him a political animal in a few years' time. The transition was marked, for Archie left an almost all black junior high to go to Los Angeles' Hamilton High School, located in west L.A., where the students came mostly from liberal, upper-middle-class Jewish families.

"It was the worst three years of my life," says Archie about his days at Hamilton. He encountered a two-headed monster in trying to deal with the problems of adjusting culturally and academically to his new environment. "I didn't dig the school. You find out that there is a difference between the way black and white people do things." Academically he found that he was ill-prepared to deal with the subject matter at Hamilton as effectively as his white classmates. "I had to work twice as hard as the white kids just to keep up."

Archie was an excellent athlete at Hamilton, starring in varsity football and track, and with hard work he was

18

able to hold good academic grades. He went from Hamilton to Los Angeles City College, a junior college, in 1966.

At LACC Archie played varsity football and ran track. He selected History and Literature as his college majors. A friend at LACC, Art Jones, who was later to go to jail with Archie for participating in the San Fernando Valley State College revolt of November 4, 1968, remembers how Archie still hadn't become politically defined despite his frustrations and bitterness from the Hamilton experience.

"Archie was not thinking about blackness and black people per se. I can remember when the Black Student Union first started at LACC, and I can recall what we all said about them, Archie also. 'What are them niggers trying to do, what are they talking about; let's just keep away from them niggers, all they're trying to do is cause trouble.' So Archie, myself, and most of the black students were doing all we could *not* to get involved with those radical people."

In the fall of '67, his sophomore year, Archie transferred from LACC to San Fernando Valley State College. He had been given a scholarship to play football, and was to enjoy an outstanding season as defensive halfback.

Eddie Dancer and Robert "Uwezo" Lewis came to San Fernando Valley State College a year later, in the fall of '68. Both were nineteen years old when they arrived at the Northridge campus, and both were in that first wave of black students to enter the college under the newly instituted Educational Opportunity Program (EOP). The EOP on the SF Valley State campus was part of a master statewide EOP designed by the California State College

19

Board of Trustees and the University of California Board of Regents to increase the black student enrollment at state-supported colleges and universities. Dancer and Lewis, as other EOP students, were given financial assistance, and the admission requirements were made more flexible for them.

Eddie Dancer was born and raised in Leveland, Texas. After finishing high school in Leveland, he was offered basketball scholarships to attend West Texas State, Morgan State, and Michigan State University. Instead of going to one of these schools, Eddie decided to come to California. He chose SF Valley State under the EOP, taking an English Literature major, with plans to continue in law school after graduation.

Talking about his life before SF Valley State, Dancer recalls: "We were always very poor. There were two children in the family, I have an older brother. I went to a small school in Leveland, George Washington Carver. It was a combination grade school-high school, and it was the black school in town. It was across the tracks from the big white high school, and our facilities were so bad that we didn't even have a gym in the school where we could play ball, or equipment for science classes, or anything like that.

"I was in the ninth grade when integration came to Leveland. They closed down our school and moved us across the tracks to the white school. I remember it was my first exposure to how white people basically consider blacks inferior, because most of the black teachers lost their jobs, and a few of our best black teachers were hired at the white high school, but as clerical workers, not teachers.

"I felt economically exploited very young, although I didn't relate to it in a political sense until I was at Valley State. I worked in the fields picking cotton in the summer, from sun-up to sun-down. It was very hard work and very little money. During the school year, they would let the blacks out of school early, and a truck would come around in front of the school to pick us up and take us to the cotton fields. We would work until dark. The black students at the high school had to do this during the school year to make money, so you can see that we had very little time to study and get good grades.

"I guess the most important thing I did while in Leveland was to play basketball in my senior year in high school. I was good, the best player on the team. We won the state championship, and I made all-state. The player closest to me in ability was also black, a fellow named Garrett. Both of us were nominated for captain of the team, early in the season. They made Garrett the captain, and it was common knowledge, some of the players even said it, that the reason was that Garrett was light—almost white—and I was dark."

When Dancer left high school he had an offer to play with the Dallas Chapperals basketball team, but he decided to go to Los Angeles instead. "I had heard those myths about California being like a promised land," he remembers. "I had an aunt out here, and I stayed with her. I wanted to go to school, so I approached certain coaches about a basketball scholarship. The coach at Valley State gave me a try out, and then offered me a basketball scholarship. That was in the summer of '68.

"I was going to accept the basketball scholarship. I

was on campus one day that summer, and I ran into Archie Chatman. We got to talking, and I told him about how I was coming to Valley State that fall on a basketball scholarship. He told me I was making a mistake, that most black brothers come to white schools with illusions of being great stars, then get exploited for their abilities while the school makes money and gains prestige, and then the school lets the brother out on his own and he doesn't have the academic training he needs to make it in the world. Archie recommended that I enter the EOP program, take some meaningful subjects, and come into Valley State on my own terms.

"It made sense. I went around with Archie and checked out the EOP. I liked what I saw, so I entered Valley State in September '68, as an EOP freshman."

Robert Lewis was born in Los Angeles. He went to San Fernando High School, not far from the Northridge campus. It was in high school that Robert joined Ron Karenga's black-nationalist-oriented US organization and took on the Swahili name "Uwezo," which means "power." Uwezo worked two years organizing in the Los Angeles black community after his graduation from San Fernando High School in '65, before entering SF Valley State in fall '68. During that period he married, and his wife Mshagishi bore him two children, a son named Kisassi and a daughter named Tonduwei.

Uwezo was converted to organized black nationalism at seventeen: "It was in 1965, and I was in my final semester at San Fernando High School. I was on my way to San Diego, with two other black brothers, to a professional baseball try-out. I was wild in those days, and on our way down to San Diego I was doing what I always did. I was smoking reefers, dropping reds [a barbiturate], and drinking wine. We were really high. We had an accident, ran into another car, and caroomed off into a tree. It almost killed the three of us.

"I was put in a hospital in San Diego. While I was there my aunt brought me a book called *The Quotable Ron Karenga*. It was a small book, with quotes on black nationalism. For instance there was a quote which said: 'The only thing that saved you from the fate of Medgar Evers was not your politics but your absence.'

"The book was talking about black. It was talking about black people, concepts, ideas—like I had never heard it being talked about before. I didn't really understand what Karenga was talking about, but it left an impression upon me.

"When I was in the hospital I began to let my hair grow. I had an Afro by the time I got out of the hospital and went back to Pacoima [a heavily black community near S.F. Valley State]. Bill Burwell had organized a group called "Afro-Pac," which was abbreviated from Afro-Pacoima, and approached me about joining the organization. I guess they were attracted to me because I was the only young black brother in Pacoima with a bush hair style. I joined their organization.

"Afro-Pac brought Karenga to Pacoima to speak in the fall of '65. Karenga's organization, US, was just getting started then, but they had tight discipline. They came to Pacoima, and they were uniformly dressed in bubas [African togas] and walked in formation. I was impressed by this.

EARL ANTHONY

"When Karenga spoke, he really impressed me. He was talking about Jesus as a faggot, and Mary as a whore, and all sorts of things about the white man. The brothers and sisters out there in the park were screaming, they loved it. Every minute in that park that day, I thought something or sombody was going to strike that man dead for talking like that. But it didn't happen, and I was really impressed then. I thought he was invulnerable. I had never heard anybody talk like that, against the white man, and the symbols of the white culture—like Christianity—and get away with it.

"I joined Karenga's US organization. Karenga brought me around. He taught me black culture and politics and gave me a positive life-style. I gave up smoking reefers, and dropping pills, and drinking wine. I took up Swahili and karate. I started using a Swahili name I was given, Uwezo, because the name fitted the way I felt about myself and the black man, and my slave name, Robert Lewis, meant nothing to me.

"I split with Karenga in '67 for reasons I don't want to go into. I started my own organization in Pacoima, called the House of Umoja. Umoja means unity in Swahili. I named it the House of Umoja because I believe unity among blacks is the first principle in black nationalism. The House of Umoja was like a black cultural and political community center. We would have counseling on the evils of dope addiction, teach brothers and sisters from the community how to shoot a gun, and go out and pick weeds from a black family's house if they needed it.

"Well, the pigs kept raiding our house under the pretext that we were organizing for a riot, or something. They also intimidated the small black businessmen around us, making them feel our activities were a threat to them. These black businessmen reacted, they became our enemies, and we found ourselves isolated.

"It was around '68 when we were forced to temporarily close the House of Umoja. I decided I would go to college, and I went to Valley State, because it was the college closest to my community."

On January 28, 1970, nineteen black students from the Black Student Union at San Fernando Valley State were sentenced in the Superior Court of Los Angeles County (Van Nuys division), the Honorable Judge Mark Brandler presiding, on charges of conspiring to commit assault, false imprisonment, and kidnapping. They were sentenced for their individual roles in the BSU's occupation of the San Fernando Valley State College Administration Building on November 4, 1968. The building had been occupied for approximately four hours, until the acting President of the college, Dr. Paul Blomgren, signed a document promising the black students eleven educational reforms plus amnesty for the occupation of the building. . . .

Archie, Eddie, and Uwezo received the stiffest sentences, the most extreme punitive action brought against any student as the result of a campus protest in the annals of American law. Each was sentenced to one to twenty-five years in the California State Prison system.

Coming to SF
Valley State

Northridge is a community in Los Angeles County, in the San Fernando Valley, twenty-five minutes from downtown Los Angeles. San Fernando Valley State College dominates Northridge. Originally, the college was to be built in Pacoima, the predominantly black and Mexican-American community to the south of Northridge in the San Fernando Valley, but the plans fell through, and in '60 San Fernando Valley State College was opened in suburban, middle-class, conservative—and almost all-white—Northridge.

California has a vast public higher education system of state colleges and universities. The University of California, with branches in many California cities and smaller communities, takes the academic cream graduating from

27

high schools, students who can't afford to go to private schools, or don't wish to. It is headed by an appointed Board of Regents. The California State Colleges handle the rest of the graduating high school seniors who still want to attend a four-year school in the state and can qualify. The California State College system is overseen by an appointed Board of Trustees. The Governor of California sits on the Board of Trustees, as well as on the University of California's Board of Regents, and both Boards are appointed to terms in office by the state administration.

San Fernando Valley State College has a sprawling campus with ultra-modern architecture which gives it a clinical look far different from the stereotyped ivy-covered campuses of the East. Most students come to SF Valley State because it is close to where they live, and like other schools in the statewide public educational system it is inexpensive. The tuition at Valley State (as of 1970) is $140 a year.

Student activism in California began at the University of California at Berkeley in '64, with the Free Speech Movement. It was a movement oriented to educational reforms deemed necessary by the radical white students of the FSM. San Francisco State College in '67 saw the beginning of the black student movement in California, an attempt to make that institution of higher learning more relevant to the black experience.

When Archie Chatman came to San Fernando Valley State in February 1967 to major in History, there were only thirty black students out of a student population of eighteen thousand. There was no black activism on campus, in fact there were no signs of even a collective feeling of black consciousness on the black students' part. When a group of black students got together on campus, it would be to play cards and socialize. As one black student told me: "Most of the brothers out there wanted to get out of school, maybe get some of those white girls out there, you know, that type of thing."

By then Chatman was militant, not in the political manner which was later to become his style, but in the same sense that he drew a hard line in his relations with whites. Les Johns, who came from LACC to Valley State with Archie in the spring of '67, also to play football, relates an example: "Archie had an enlarged photograph in his dormitory room. It was taken at a football game, and Archie had his arm around this white boy's neck. Underneath the picture he had an inscription, 'My name is Archie Chatman. I don't answer to "boy," and I don't eat watermelon.' "

This tough attitude of Chatman's was a necessary emotional defense against the hostility of his environment at Valley State. To a person, black students who were there in '67 and '68 say that the Administration, faculty, and students made them feel at best ill at ease, and at worst unwanted. As black Valley State co-ed Teresa Tolliver expressed it: "I came to this school in good faith and I did not know what racism really was until I came. . . . I didn't have any hatred in my heart for white people . . . what I felt upon entering San Fernando Valley State College was isolation . . . being there as a black student set me apart."

In the fall of '67, Chatman played football at Valley State. He played defensive halfback, ran back kickoffs and punts, and sometimes played flankerback on offense. Until he broke his arm in the sixth game of the season, he played first team.

Les Johns and Art Jones were not as fortunate. The football coaches played Johns and Jones very rarely, and certain things they did made the three of them, the only blacks on the team, come to the conclusion that the coaches were racist. Art Jones puts it bluntly: "In practice they would always put Les and me against each other in man to man. I guess it was 'Let's see the niggers kill each other.'

"There were other examples, like the Junior Rose Bowl. We played West Texas State. Les had played between first and second string all year. They didn't even play him in the Junior Rose Bowl. They played a white boy who hadn't played all year because he had been injured. Later, when we confronted the coaches and Athletic Director with this, the head football coach said they had played the white boy because it was the game of his life. Like Les didn't have a life."

In the fall of '67, the black students at Valley State were beginning to come out of their lethargy. Bill Burwell, a sociology major, and Jerome Walker, a psychology major, began to approach black students with the idea of forming a black student union. Burwell and Walker were from the nearby black community of Pacoima and had been organizing there. At that time, they were the most politically aware blacks at Valley State, and they had correctly assessed that black students at their campus would be willing to get in step with the rising militancy of black students at white-dominated institutions across the country (militancy by black students against black institutions of higher learning had begun the year before).

The first two black student organizers that Burwell and Walker recruited were Chatman and Genie Washington, a young black co-ed. The four of them managed to swell their ranks to twenty-five within a few weeks (which meant that nearly all the black students on campus had been enlisted).

It takes twenty-five members to apply for a charter as an on-campus organization. When the Black Student Union had the quota, it applied. The charter was granted in November '67.

The infant BSU wasted no time in developing a program. On-campus meetings were held once a week, every Tuesday. They dealt with the problems facing the black students at Valley State and reinforced the organization of the BSU in those formative months.

One major decision was to concentrate BSU efforts in Pacoima. The BSU accepted the premise that work in the black community would be more relevant and necessary to them than working to force change at the college; that the gut-level problems of black existence were in the community.

Their focus was on the black youth of Pacoima. Classes were held in three categories: (1) self-defense, (2) culture, and (3) political education, and BSU members as well as non-student blacks from Pacoima participated.

Karate classes were given in the self-defense category. In culture, classes were given in Swahili, the national language in a few East African countries and increasingly the political *lingua franca* throughout Africa. And in political education classes, the works of great black leaders and thinkers such as Kwame Nkrumah, Malcolm X, W.E.B. DuBois, and Frantz Fanon were read and discussed.

Chatman talked about the initial excursion of the BSU into the Pacoima black community in fall '67: "The BSU's link with the Pacoima community was through Afro-Pac. Afro-Pac had been started by Bill Burwell a couple of years before he came to Valley State. Jerome Walker was an important member of Afro-Pac. When Burwell and Walker came to Valley State they organized the BSU. They were more familiar with the black experience than the rest of us black students on campus, at least on an organizational level. Burwell and Walker maintained their active roles in Afro-Pac, so the BSU simply used Afro-Pac as its link to the community.

"We did have problems when we first came into Pacoima. Afro-Pac was isolated from the community. They were talking about black nationalism, but the community wasn't responding. It viewed Afro-Pac as a bunch of crazy niggers trying to stir up trouble, and in general thought of the Afro-Pac–BSU alliance as more of a threat than a benefit.

"This is not difficult to understand if you examine the make-up of Pacoima. It is a large community of blacks and browns, but it is a suburban community, and the people in it labor under the illusion that they don't have the same problems as urban blacks—such as poor housing, police brutality, etc. It *is* an illusion, for they do have the same problems, but they stick their heads in the sand, and they are far enough away from the concrete politicization that occurs in urban areas to be successful in this self-delusion, and thereby remain lethargic.

"Although we were isolated when we first went to Pacoima in '67, we worked hard, trying to politicize the people. November 4, 1968 was what got us over. It is one thing to tell the people what is wrong with the system, nationally or locally; it is quite another thing for them to see a clear-cut example right in their own backyard. It affects them then.

"The black people in Pacoima never related to Valley State. They didn't go to school there, and they couldn't get jobs there. We had been pointing these things out long before November 4th. When the black students revolted on Campus on November 4th, a couple of our demands were for more black students—who the community people knew would be their sons and daughters—and for fair employment on campus. Black people from Pacoima knew we were talking about them, and the system came down so hard on us—after that we were legitimized in the black community.

"The repression by the school, police, and courts helped us in the Pacoima community as much as our own efforts. After November 4th, the community was behind us, they had become politicized. We spoke in the community daily, at rallies, or churches or schools. Community people would come to our rallies at Valley State. We had become unified. The college feared the community. They thought it was violent and irrational, and capable of doing anything after November 4th. Until then they had looked on it as docile. This is obvious by the way they have reacted, because Valley State has made many decisions after the November 4th revolt that have been favorable to black students, and we know that one of the things that the administration has taken into consideration is the fact that we have the active support of the black community of Pacoima."

The BSU also became a member of the Black Student Alliance, an organization in Los Angeles which sought to bring the various black student unions in and around that city together under one umbrella so that their actions on the campuses and in the community would be coordinated. The Black Student Alliance was only a partial success. Its most self-defeating tendency was to deal exclusively with issues and it thereby failed to develop an organizational ideology which would have in turn reinforced the organization. To a large degree the BSA remained splintered into individual BSU's focusing on issues that pertained to them rather than to a united front.

The BSU's first confrontation with the Valley State administration came in January '68. It was a meeting set up with the Athletic Director, Dr. Glen Arnett, and Head Football Coach Dr. Sam Winningham. It was held in Arnett's office, and the purpose was to discuss inequities that the BSU felt black varsity football players were subjected to, such as not being played and not getting sufficient financial grants to play football. Racial slurs allegedly made by the coaching staff were also on the agenda (it had been rumored that the coaches griped continually about the black players, and had been heard to say the team needed a "super nigger" who could run the 100-yard dash in 9.4 in his bare feet).

Representing the BSU that day were Burwell, Walker,

Jones, and Chatman. The meeting was heated, and Chatman became verbally arrogant. Arnett told Archie several times to be quiet and stop using vulgar language.

Nothing was accomplished at the meeting, and the BSU members left with the same impression of the Athletic Department as they'd had before: it was racist-oriented, and unwilling to change. The following fall the BSU and the Athletic Department, their differences representative of larger disagreements between Valley State and its black students, ran a collision course that threw that campus into the furnace of black student revolt.

Educational Opportunities Program

Many of the black student activists at San Fernando Valley State had come to the college as the result of the Educational Opportunities Program (EOP) instituted by California in 1968 at its state universities and colleges (similar programs were put into effect in other states around the same time). The purpose of the program was to develop, inside the confines of the higher education process, individuals who previously had been known, in educators' vernacular, as "low achievers," largely as a result of flaws in the lower education system.

Students accepted into the EOP were to be assisted through the first, and possibly the second, year of their stay at the college or university. The assistance was to be given in the areas of housing, financial aid (work-study, grant loans), as well as academic tutoring and personal counseling when needed.

In the spring of '68 it was announced that San Fernando Valley State (as other colleges and universities in the state) would be starting an EOP the following fall. The administration at Valley State planned to admit fifteen EOP students. The distribution would be equal between the blacks and the browns; there would be seven Afro-Americans and seven Mexican-Americans. It hadn't been decided what to do with the fifteenth student.

Walker was the chairman of the BSU at the time, and Chatman was co-chairman, having recently replaced Burwell. Chatman took the responsibility of convincing the Valley State administration and faculty that the EOP should be expanded, and that black courses for credit should be started that fall.

A BSU member said of Chatman: "He was always going to meetings with the faculty. Sometimes others in the BSU would go with him; many times he would go by himself. It was around this time that he became the dominant figure in the BSU, and it was mostly because of the pressure he put on the faculty that the EOP was expanded."

In April '68 the Valley State administration relented to Chatman's pressure. Instead of the original fifteen EOP slots, there would be 300 in the program by fall '68—150 Afro-Americans and 150 Mexican-Americans. However, the administration transferred the total responsibility of recruiting the 300 students for EOP to the BSU and UMA (United Mexican-Americans).

Out of the meetings Chatman and the other BSU students had with the faculty came another very important concession. It was agreed that four black courses for credit would be taught in the fall: Black Sociology, which was to have a white professor listed as the instructor, but was actually to be taught by Walker, a sociology major, who, because he was a student, could not have the course listed under his name; Black Psychology, taught by Burwell, a psychology major, with the same understanding; Black History taught by Herbert Hill, a white member of the Los Angeles NAACP; and Black Literature, which was also taught by a white instructor.

The Valley State administration also agreed to replace Dr. Stanley Charnofsky, a white professor who had been heading the non-white oriented EOP, with Gene Bostic, a black graduate student who was very active in the BSU. With this move, and having left the recruiting of new EOP students in the hands of the BSU, the administration and faculty in effect relinquished responsibility for the success or failure of the EOP at Valley State, thus putting themselves in a position where they could not be blamed if anything went wrong.

The BSU shouldered its huge responsibility. It organized a committee consisting of Chatman, Walker, Burwell, Johns, Genie Washington, Howard Johnson, and Bostic (other BSU members worked on the committee from time to time) to formulate criteria by which to evaluate the black high school seniors for acceptance into the EOP (UMA set up a similar evaluation system).

Motivation was the main determinant, for the BSU realized that most black high school seniors lacked the academic qualifications to enter college: they knew from the beginning that they could barely afford the luxury of high school, let alone college.

During the last two months of the spring '68 semester, the BSU recruited in every predominantly black high school in the area. The procedure was to talk to the counselors and teachers and to form a master list of students who showed potential. The BSU committee then talked to these students individually. It was a time-consuming process, for out of the more than one thousand black students who showed potential, and were interviewed, the list had to be narrowed down to only 150 EOP slots. By June the BSU (as well as UMA) had completed the task of selecting the EOP students.

While doing research for this book in Los Angeles in June '70, I decided I wanted to know more about the program that had been such a crucial element in bringing the black activists to the Valley State campus. I talked to Jerry Crawford, a twenty-nine-year-old black man who had recently taken over for Bostic as co-director of the Afro-American component of the Educational Opportunities Program. Originally from Washington, D.C., Crawford had graduated from SF Valley State with a B.A. in sociology in '65. He talked to me at length about the problems and successes of the EOP in its two-year history at Valley State, as well as of the changes at Valley State since his student days there.

One of the first questions I asked Crawford was whether the methods of recruiting for the EOP had changed much since its first summer.

Crawford was careful in phrasing his answer. "Basically we're using the same technique—because they knew what they were doing in '68. We've simply polished the technique."

"Tell me how you recruited the black EOP freshman for the '70–'71 school year at Valley State," I asked.

"We had a recruitment team of five black EOP students. We used these students because they were products of the program, and because they were young and not that far removed from high schools. Therefore they could relate to the transition that high school students would have to make.

"Thanks to Archie Chatman, Bill Burwell, and the others who were running the BSU in '68 and first started this EOP recruitment process, we have now established contacts with the black high schools in the Los Angeles City and County area. So they knew about us and our program when we went around to the high schools and talked to the students, usually in an auditorium where all the seniors had gathered. We gave them details about our program, our admission standards . . ."

"What were those admission standards," I interrupted.

"First, a senior must have a letter from his high school, usually from his senior counselor, recommending him. Then he must have two letters of recommendation from community residents: a minister, an employer, or anybody who can give valuable insight into what type of person he is. Then he must write an autobiography telling us about his ambitions, his family background, and things of that sort. There is no set form for the autobiography, it's a personal statement. What we look for in the autobiography is where the student's head is at. Then we examine his high school grade transcript and his scores on his college boards, SAT or ACT. There is no set pattern as to how these five elements are weighed; we try to get a balanced picture of the person applying."

"It must be difficult to make the final selection."

"It is. We had 1600 applications for the Afro-American component of the EOP for the '70–'71 year. We had only four hundred slots. I'm not that familiar with the process for the Mexican-American component.

"Anyway," he continued, "after a committee made up of myself, the five EOP students, and a member of the Afro-American Student Union screened the applicants, we made our selections. Then these four hundred incoming black students, plus the four hundred incoming Chicano students selected by the United Mexican-Americans, went before a joint black-brown review board. This board was made up of one faculty member from Afro-American Studies, one from Mexican-American Studies, a representative of the Mexican-American Student Union, a black EOP student, a brown EOP student, and a representative from the Admissions Office, who has to be there because of state regulations, and the co-directors of the EOP, Mike Verdugo [of Mexican-American Studies] and myself. This was actually a personal interview before acceptance of the EOP student."

"Did this review board turn anybody down?"

"No, because the Afro-American component, and the Mexican-Americans also, had already made their decisions. The representative from the Admissions Office has never been negative about our selections—he is more or less there because of procedure. We have autonomy."

"OK, then what happened?" I asked.

"We sent the students a preliminary acceptance and an appointment before the board of the Admissions Office. This is state and federal regulation. The Admissions Office board has never turned down one of our recommendations in the three years of the program's existence. Then the students received their final acceptance. The entire process took five months. We began in April in high schools, and constantly worked at it until final acceptance of this year's four hundred in the latter part of August."

California being a hotbed of conservatism and reaction, and the EOP being geared almost exclusively to blacks and browns, there has been active and vocal opposition to the program. The Coordinating Council on Higher Education (CCHE) funded a study to examine and evaluate the EOP. Based on the program's first year in operation ('68), the report, known as "The Kitano Report," came to the conclusion that the EOP was "ineffective." The report has served as a rationale for a few state legislators to propose bills that would either trim the EOP budget or cut out the program entirely.

"It was clear to us from the beginning of this program," Jerry Crawford told me, "that Governor Reagan and the conservative state of California were not going to allocate the type of budget that would give this experiment a fair chance at success."

The California state budget allocation for the EOP program in '70 (its third year in operation) was $300,000 for all state colleges and universities. The federal five-to-one matching grant was 1.5 million. Valley State's total share was $312,000, and that was to finance a program that had 400 returning black students, 375 returning Mexican-

American students, 400 incoming black students, and 350 incoming Mexican-American students. This amounted to a total of 1575 black and brown EOP students for the '70–'71 academic year at the Northridge campus.

The budget allocation of $312,000 was basically designed to take care of the personnel salaries, the supplies, and other overhead items. Very little of this money went to the 1575 black and brown students for furthering their individual academic careers. Crawford would like to see the state make a far more substantial contribution. "If the state would increase their share by at least five times, and with the five-to-one federal matching grant, then there would be money in the budget at Valley State to give the desperately needed financial aid to black and brown students, almost all of whom come from low-income, poverty-level homes."

Most of the financial aid to the black and brown EOP students comes from a federally funded work-study program. Each department or on-campus organization that has a budget usually gives priority to EOP students when hiring student help—the department or organization only has to pay 20 per cent of the salary, and the federal government pays the other 80 per cent.

I asked Crawford: "Do you think the work-study program is sufficient to your needs?"

"No, I don't," he answered sharply. "The maximum time an EOP student can work under the program is fifteen hours a week. The maximum pay is $2.25 per hour, and very few make that. You have to realize that most of our students are products of the ghetto—and are taken out of

44

that environment and put into a strange and hostile one, the affluent Northridge community. This makes for a difficult adjustment in their life style at a very young age, and then you compound the problem by having them work for their education. The reason they are there in the first place is because they are poor, and black or brown, and American society has discriminated against them by giving them an education in the ghettoes which is markedly inferior to the education of middle-class whites. . . .

"So you take these young EOP students, who are in this hostile environment, who have had an inferior education because they were born black or brown, and have them work to support their way through school, when their relatively affluent white counterparts at Valley State, who are much more advanced in reading, math, etc., only have to go to class. You can see how the system, even with programs like the EOP, makes a black man work twice as hard, with everything against him from the beginning."

"Are there other alternatives for a black or brown EOP student who needs the money to finance his education?" I asked.

"First, *all* the EOP students need the money. You have to realize that EOP students have to carry a full academic load, at least twelve units a semester. Some of them will take out loans, such as National Defense Loans. But you have to pay those loans back right after you graduate, so you start off your post-graduate career with a huge debt, and if you don't graduate you're in bigger trouble because you have the debt, and your earning potential is much less. To a seventeen-year-old black or brown entering college, and told that in four years he will have to repay $10,000—more money than he can really imagine—it's a turn-off. It discourages him from the beginning."

"But so far, going into its third year, you feel the EOP has been a success, despite the obstacles?"

"It definitely has," Crawford said. "Over the last two years, the average disqualification rate among the entire student population at Valley State has been 15 to 20 per cent per year. For that same period, the disqualification rate among black EOP students has been less than 5 per cent. Last year, '69–'70, only 23 out of 411 black students in the EOP were disqualified because of grades, and the requirements are stiffer than for other students. You have to maintain a 2.0 average in order not to be dropped from school on the EOP program, whereas a regular student can stay in school with a 1.0 average. [The grading system has 4.0 as a perfect grade, 2.0 as average, and 0.0 as failing.] And remember these black EOP students, according to the college and university admission system prior to '68, were not supposed to have been college material, and now they are sitting in classes with white students who have had calculus, chemistry, and other advanced subjects that the EOP students never had the opportunity or incentive to take, and are doing better than those students.

"Even the argument used by certain politicians and educators that much of the beefing up of the grade averages of EOP students comes because they take comparatively soft Afro-American Studies courses goes nowhere. The course material in Afro-American Studies at this campus is

46

definitely not remedial, and the grading is as stiff as, if not stiffer than, the grading in other departments."

"As you see it then, what is the reason for the better overall performance of the black EOP students as compared to their white counterparts?" I asked.

"Dedication and commitment. These kids have a remarkable maturity for seventeen, or eighteen, or nineteen year olds, a maturity reinforced by their sense of responsibility. The disqualification level would be even lower if it wasn't for the overwhelming personal problems—such as money, or transportation. For instance, there is no bus system that runs from the black-brown communities of Pacoima and LA. So a black or brown student is making a fifty-mile round trip every day, unless he pays out money to live on campus. The white students live right in Northridge—a community with an average family income of more than $10,000 a year—and they have cars. For some reason they didn't build the college in Pacoima as they had first planned. I will simply say that it still amazes me that young black students are much more mature and better balanced than young white students.

"The EOP program was offered by whites on this campus with the expectation that if they gave us a free hand we would fail, and then they could say, 'I told you so.' That first summer program in June '68 was funded by a $98,000 Office of Economic Opportunities grant—to prepare *300* incoming black and brown EOP students for their academic careers at Valley State.

"The only thing that has saved the program on this campus," Crawford concluded, "and other black people in

47

the administration of EOPs around California say pretty much the same thing, has been the dedication and commitment of the students. I'm talking now about the black component of EOP on this campus, with which I'm most familiar. The inspiration for the dedication and commitment among the blacks on this campus comes from the Valley State 19 [the BSU students who were sentenced to various prison and probationary sentences for participating in the November 4, 1968 revolt at SF Valley State]. The incoming students—and this may sound a little romantic, but it's true—feel that they have an individual commitment to 'the 19' to make good at this college, because those students sacrificed themselves to give them a chance."

November 4, 1968

In the fall of '68 Chatman made a decision: he would not play any more football for Valley State. (He also influenced Jones and Johns to give up football, so there were no longer any blacks on the varsity.) This lost him his scholarship, but it allowed him to devote his energies to making his tenure as Chairman of the BSU an effective one. In Archie's cabinet that fall semester were Howard Johnson as co-chairman, Rosalyn Emory as Treasurer, and Genie Washington as Secretary.

Chatman was busy from the first day of the fall semester, for the BSU now had the additional 150 EOP students (most of whom he had worked with as an instructor in the summer program). Among other activities, he was holding rap sessions in black political education in

Northridge Hall, where most of the black EOP students lived. Many of these had also begun to work actively as members of BSU, and a few were to play major roles in the black student revolt of November 4.

Foremost among these was Robert Uwezo Lewis, the nineteen-year-old freshman who had been a black activist in the Los Angeles community since he was sixteen. Uwezo became head of security for the BSU, and among other things taught karate to the members. Then there was Eddie Dancer, the freshman from Leveland, Texas, who had been a high school All American basketball player. And Sheldon Jones, seventeen years old when he entered Valley State, whose commitment to the struggle for black people was to be so solidified by his experience on that campus that he would later repeatedly make the statement "I am a revolutionary," despite the fact that he faced a stiff prison sentence for his part in November 4th.

There were many others, and their presence charged the already explosive racial situation on the conservative campus. It was almost inevitable that the Athletic Department, which had been the center of controversy the year before when the BSU had accused it of racial inequities toward black varsity football players, would create the incident that brought the BSU and the administration into open antagonism.

Although there were no black players on the varsity, there were three on the freshman football team. George Boswell was one of them.

On October 17, 1968, the San Fernando Valley State freshman football team played the frosh from California Poly of San Luis Obispo. It was a night game, played at

Northridge, and twenty or more members of the BSU (including Chatman) watched the game together.

During the second half a fracas developed between one of Valley State's black players and three players from Cal Poly. It seemed to Boswell that no one was going to help the brother, so he ran from the bench to where the action was, but by the time he arrived the officials had things under control.

Donald Markham, the freshman football coach, quickly followed Boswell onto the field. Boswell says that the coach told him to run off the field, but he decided he would walk rather than run as Markham had commanded. Markham lost control. "He grabbed me around the neck," says Boswell, "turned me around, and kicked me in the groin." Boswell then went to the sidelines, took off his helmet, shoulder pads, and jersey—and quit the team on the spot.

The BSU students at the game were infuriated by the kicking incident. Later, they went en masse to the Valley State locker room to get an explanation from Coach Markham. Markham was belligerent, and emotions got heated that night in the locker room. The white frosh team members, backing up their coach, began a fight with the BSU members (as one black student put it, "We were able to kick those faggot white boys' asses").

The next day, October 18, the BSU called an emergency meeting. It was decided that the BSU would ask the Athletic Director to fire Coach Markham (Markham was a volunteer coach, and therefore the bureaucratic problems of firing a faculty member with tenure would be avoided).

Dr. Stanley Charnofsky, a faculty member in close

touch with the BSU, was approached to serve as an inter-
mediary with Athletic Director Arnett. Charnofsky accepted, and expressed to Dr. Arnett the BSU's desire to
meet with him and two faculty members.

A meeting was set for Monday, November 4th at 11
A.M., in the Athletic Director's office. Arnett told Charnofsky that he expected three representatives of the BSU to
meet with him and two other faculty members.

When Charnofsky told Chatman of the November
4th meeting, he omitted the important condition that three
members of the BSU would meet with three members of the
faculty. Chatman immediately informed his full BSU constituency of the meeting, stating that the issue to be discussed was their demand that frosh coach Donald Markham
be fired at once.

On November 4th, at about 10 A.M., Charnofsky
reminded Chatman of the meeting and for the first time
told him of the condition that only three BSU members be
present. The entire BSU membership was already assembled
at the organization's campus office, primed for the confrontation with Arnett.

Chatman's hands were tied, for as Attorney Morgan
Moten explained later in his defense of Archie at the trial:
"Since '54 black people have been afraid even of other
black people because we've had too many sell-outs." Chatman's leadership of the BSU would have been endangered
if at this point he had announced that only three BSU members out of the hundred or more that had gathered would
be able to meet with Arnett. He decided to continue with
the plan for a mass confrontation.

Chatman led the BSU over to the Athletic Director's

office. Backing up Arnett at the meeting were Charnofsky and the varsity football coach Winningham.

From the beginning the meeting was tense. Arnett refused to discuss BSU's demand before the full membership. His explanation was that at past meetings with large numbers of BSU members present, he and other members of the faculty had not had a chance to talk, and that generally nothing had been accomplished.

The BSU compromised, and only Chatman, Dancer, and Uwezo went into the Athletic Director's office. The rest of the BSU students waited in the conference room.

It had been almost a year since Chatman and the BSU had had their initial confrontation with Arnett and the Athletic Department, and relations had deteriorated to a point where now, in Arnett's office that morning of November 4th, there was a feeling of armed truce.

Arnett started in a bitter tone. "Archie, you called this meeting, what do you want?"

"I want you to prepare a statement announcing the firing of the freshman football coach, Donald Markham, and sign it," said Chatman firmly.

"I cannot, and I will not, fire him. What else do you want?" Arnett was unyielding, as he had always been in his relations with Chatman and the BSU.

From that point, the hostility between the two negotiating parties escalated. At one point during the negotiations, Dr. Byrne C. Fernelius, Chairman of the Recreation Department, was walking past Arnett's office. Later at the trial he was to say of that morning: "I heard shouts and people banging tables. I feared for Arnett, Charnofsky, and Winningham."

Fernelius summoned Captain George Munze, head of the campus security police. Munze checked the situation out and obviously felt there was no cause for alarm, for he told Fernelius, "Let me know if anything develops," and left. Fernelius then entered the Athletic Director's office to join his comrades.

After many heated exchanges, Arnett finally told Chatman that he was powerless to fire Coach Markham. He said the only man who could do that was Acting President Paul B. Blomgren, and it was decided to continue the discussion in President Blomgren's office in the Administration Building.

As Chatman recalled: "When we went over to the Administration Building that day we were only concerned with making one demand of the President, that freshman football coach Don Markham be fired for kicking the black football player. That kicking incident had been the latest and most overt example of racism that black students had been subjected to on the campus, and the emotional response to it by the black students was the catalytic force that moved us into action.

"When, predictably, Arnett and Winningham continued to act like the faculty at Valley State had always acted toward us by stating in effect that they intended to do nothing about it, we were determined not to let it go at that. We were determined to be heard and to get some reasonable explanation why Markham should not be fired. So we went over to the Administration Building."

It is 700 yards from the Athletic Department to the Administration Building. That morning in November, Drs. Charnofsky, Fernelius, Arnett, and Winningham walked those 700 yards flanked by 100 or more members of the BSU (many of the BSU members wore sweatshirts emblazoned with their slogan, "By Any Means Necessary," taken from the words of Malcolm X).

At the trial, the prosecution was to call this trek from the Athletic Department to the Administration Building a "forced walk," which became the basis for the kidnapping charge (the BSU denied this accusation, as well as another that they walked in military formation).

Two isolated incidents occurred during the walk to the Administration Building. Dancer was involved in both. He slapped a white student because "He kept antagonizing me by saying I was acting like a 'white Mississippi cop' "; and he punched another white student, who he said "kept insulting us by pushing one of the black students off the walk, and ordering us to march in a column."

When they arrived at the Administration Building they took the stairs to the fifth floor where the President's office is located. By this time the emotions of the BSU members had become exacerbated.

Art Jones described that feeling: "I guess it was like a dog you keep on a chain. Once that dog gets free it runs wild. I guess that's the way we were on the fifth floor. We didn't want to hurt anybody, but then we were tired of taking shit from the people at Valley State. We took over the fifth floor. We moved all the staff into one room. The young brothers were running up and down the hall just letting off steam, waiting for Archie and the others to work out the plan on how to fire Markham. The sisters were in the room watching the staff."

The fifth floor of the Administration Building at Valley

State is set aside for the top brass. All administrators and clerical staff, thirty-seven in all, were herded into room 509, the President's conference room. Chatman, Uwezo, and Dancer, and from time to time a few other BSU students, were in the office of Vice President of Administrative Affairs Harold Spencer. Spencer was there, along with Arnett and Winningham, and everyone was waiting for President Blomgren to appear.

"When we got into the Administration Building," said Chatman, "and while we were trying to locate the president, we were talking among ourselves. We came to the obvious conclusion that we had the opportunity this time to confront the policy makers—the administration —with the major problems facing black students at that campus, problems which had developed because of the racist-oriented nature of Valley State. It was an excellent opportunity, for the administration wasn't in a position to procrastinate, they had to deal with the problem then. So we worked up a list of twelve demands."

Only a handful of students had ever seen the Acting President, and unbeknownst to the BSU he had been put in room 509 with the rest of the staff. At one point, when a discussion arose among black students as to the whereabouts of the President, Blomgren stepped forward and said, "I am the President." There was laughter among the students, and one warned: "Shaddup, and get up against the wall, white muthafucka. And don't you say nuthin'."

It was understandable that the young black students should be hostile to any white person's assertion of authority. A few minutes earlier, a Los Angeles undercover policeman, who had shown credentials as a member of the

Los Angeles press to gain access to the fifth floor, had left the premises flashing his badge and waving his pistol at nearby BSU members.

Once word of the occupation of the fifth floor circulated around the campus, counter actions were started. The electricity was cut off, making things uncomfortable without lights, air conditioning, and elevators (the BSU enforced a no-smoking decree, so that it would not become too stuffy).

Students for a Democratic Society (SDS) and a couple of dozen members of Faculty for Democratic Institutions (both Valley State affiliates) had called a class walkout for 11:30 A.M. that same day to support the BSU's demand that Coach Markham be fired. Along with a couple of hundred followers, they were having a rally in the Open Forum (an outside space set aside for public debate), when they heard about the BSU occupation of the Administration Building and went over to show their support for the black students.

Mike Lee, a leader of the campus SDS, went up to the fifth floor to confer with Chatman and the BSU leaders. By this time Blomgren had been identified and was in Spencer's office listening to the BSU demand that Markham be fired. Blomgren suggested that the BSU present their list of demands. "When the President was located," Chatman recalled, "we showed him the demands, and realizing we meant business, he consented to sit down and assist us in putting them in a formal style."

Lee went downstairs to the front of the building, where over three hundred students had gathered. One hundred members of the Los Angles Police Department had also assembled, ready for the command to move in. SDS decided to occupy the first two floors of the Administration Building, which had been cleared. (Sixteen white radicals from SDS were later arrested for the occupation of the first two floors. They were charged with misdemeanors, in contrast to the felony charges given the BSU.)

Going to the roof of the Administration Building, Lee began to hold an open discussion with the students below as to the merits of the BSU demands. He was using a bullhorn. The students in front of the Administration Building had another bullhorn, and were voicing rebuttals to the radical Lee. Associated Students President Glenn Mahler later said vehemently: "The BSU had not gone through all the proper channels and these so-called Columbias don't work."

Inside the office of Vice President Spencer, oblivious to the tumult outside, Chatman and three of his aides, and Blomgren and the four faculty members, together worked out a list of BSU demands for educational reforms which, when implemented by the Administration and Faculty, would make the environment at Valley State healthy and workable for black students.

The final draft of the demands reads:

1. *Black Studies Department leading to a B.A. degree*
2. *Recruitment of 500 black students per year until racial population of the college becomes consistent with the national racial averages*
3. *Tutorial facilities to be operated by BSU to aid EOP students with study skills*

4. *No on Title V, and have college and Black Studies representatives at meetings which are to be held concerning Title V*
5. *Investigation of employment practices on campus*
6. *Investigation of Black Faculty for Black Studies Department (50 per cent black students, 50 per cent faculty committee to choose)*
7. *Disarming of campus police*
8. *Set up grievance board by which students can bring grievances against faculty members*
9. *Fire Coach Markham*
10. *Conduct an investigation on Athletic Director Arnett; meanwhile Arnett to be removed from teaching duties*
11. *Weekly meetings with President to make sure these grievances are met promptly and receive the maximum college support*

Chatman had some thoughtful reasons for the demands. "In drawing up the list, we did not concentrate exclusively on demands that affected black students on the campus," he said, "but we also included demands that affected the black people in the Pacoima community. We did this because we realized that the college was also practicing racism toward the black community, and by including these demands we would be able to gather support in the community.

"For instance, one of our demands was that there be an investigation of the employment practices on campus. The college was close to the black community of Pacoima, yet very few black people from that community had jobs at the college, and many needed work. On the other hand, those blacks employed on campus were *under*employed. In one case we knew of, a brother with three years of college was being supervised by a white boy with less than an eighth-grade education, who probably couldn't spell his name. There was another case of a brother who was suspended from his job because he frequently talked to us.

"Most of the demands were obviously needed. Take for example the one for disarming the campus police. Almost all of the black students at the college are from the ghetto, and have experienced or seen examples of police brutality. Then they come to this campus and the campus police are armed. It was an example of the racist nature of the college that when the large number of black students were enrolled under the EOP in fall '68 there was a large build-up of campus police. I would say they at least doubled their force. Northridge Hall, where most of these black EOP students lived, was the heaviest guarded place on campus.

"Another example of something that was obviously needed was a grievance board whereby students could bring their complaints before the faculty. We had no way to express ourselves to the faculty except by our own direct action. A couple of times that fall, faculty members had made derogatory remarks about black women, concerning sexual diseases—taking things out of context. The BSU had to march into the instructors' classes and confront these teachers on the spot. A couple of times we even had to throw faculty members out of our meetings when they refused to leave after we had told them to. If there had been a grievance board we would not have had to resort to these forms of direct action.

"Our major concerns were concentrated in four demands: that a Black Studies Department be started on the campus; that five hundred black students a year be recruited to go to school at Valley State, until we had a proportionate racial average; that black faculty be recruited to instruct in the Black Studies Department; and that there be tutorial services at Valley State for black students, run by black students.

"We needed the Black Studies Department as a positive alternative for black students on campus, because the college was racist oriented and didn't relate to us. However, we had an understanding of the subtle nature of racism, and therefore knew that we had not only to bring black students on campus, we had to keep them there. We had to find ways to avoid the inherent mechanisms of a racist institution that led to failure in the past. We had to eliminate these failure mechanisms.

"The first step was to have black faculty teaching black students, thereby eliminating the individual racism that the white instructor usually has for black students. Also a black curriculum, formulated by a black faculty, which would have relevance to the black students.

"A very important final step, after establishing the Black Studies Department and recruiting the black students, is the tutorial program. The black student is an individual who is the product of eighteen years of white oppression when he enters college as a freshman. Therefore, he hasn't had the educational opportunities to develop certain skills

61

that his white counterpart has had, and even more important, his personality has usually been shattered by this experience of oppression. The tutorial program, then, has to operate on two levels. It has to equip the young black student with educational skills such as math, reading, chemistry, etc., and it also has to reconstruct the personality of that student on a positive basis, which is done by giving him a black ideology, or perspective, so that he has a foundation for his newly acquired skills.

"We realized on November 4th that all four things—black studies, large black student populace, black faculty, and black tutorial program—were needed if we were going to develop a body of black intellectuals—not Negro intellectuals—at Valley State, who would become a positive force in the black community."

By this time it was about 3 P.M., and the BSU was aware of the police lurking in front of the Administration Building, waiting for the word to move on them. For this reason they added a very important twelfth demand, which was agreed to by Blomgren and the faculty members present: *12. Amnesty to students involved in the confrontation.*

Acting President Blomgren gave his word to Chatman and his aides that he would honor the twelve demands, and he signed the list. Then Chatman and Blomgren went to the first floor to talk to people from the Los Angeles Human Rights Commission to arrange for the safety of the BSU members as they left the building (it had been rumored that along with the police, white students led by the athletes were organizing to attack BSU members).

There is a roof which juts away from the building on

the first floor of the Administration Building. Blomgren went out on it and talked to the more than 2000 students who had gathered outside. He talked of the demands, and he told of the amnesty he had granted to the BSU.

Chatman went back upstairs. He sent Uwezo down with the girls first. Then the rest of the BSU left the building from a side entrance while Blomgren was talking to the students massed out front. The BSU went unmolested. It was 4 P.M., and the Administration Building had been occupied for four hours.

The Aftermath

The day after the confrontation and occupation, the BSU held a rally at noon in the Open Forum to explain the twelve demands to the student body. The rally was well attended.

It became clear at the rally that there were going to be repercussions from November 4th. The BSU noticed several men, not television people, taking motion pictures and still photos of the black students. It was discovered later that these men were undercover police, and the pictures were going to be shown to the staff and administration who had been on the fifth floor the previous day, so that they could correlate faces and names from the students' files.

Faculty members who had rapport with the BSU approached them after the rally and told them that the police had been on campus since the evening before, and had questioned them about the participants in the confrontations. They also said that a high ranking member of the staff of Glenn S. Dumke, Chancellor of the California State College System, was on campus conducting an investigation of the previous days' activities.

From that day, November 5th, the approximately two hundred black students at Valley State began a "Black Moratorium" to show solidarity in support of the twelve demands. No black students attended classes (the moratorium lasted close to four months until most of the demands were recognized in the spring of '69).

California's local and state bureaucratic machinery made its move against the Valley State BSU the afternoon of November 5th. Governor Ronald Reagan set the tone in a television interview by stating: "The demonstrators should be dragged off by the scruff of the neck." Almost simultaneously, Los Angeles Police Chief Thomas Redding called a press conference where he announced that arrest warrants had been issued for the BSU members.

Fast on the heels of these moves, as if in capitulation to higher authority, Dr. Paul Krimel, Executive Assistant to the President of SF Valley State, made the statement: "The students showed butcher knives in ordering administration and faculty around. . . . They lectured us about how black people had been treated like pigs for four hundred years and that now we just have to get used to it."

Then came the Judas Act. Acting President Blomgren repudiated the amnesty, and called the demands he signed: "A list of terms dictated by those who had the force."

(As was the case with other liberal college and university presidents in California during this troubled time, Blomgren stepped down from his position a few months after the confrontation. This move was attributed to his diabetic condition, which had never interfered with his duties before.)

Late that afternoon members of the Los Angeles Police Department stationed themselves around Northridge Hall, where most of the BSU members lived, waiting to arrest them. The BSU, anticipating a police move against them from the information that had been circulating, had split into three groups and gone to nearby Pacoima to spend the night of the 5th at the homes of Walker, Burwell, and Bostic.

That evening, the LAPD arrested Tim Collins at his mother's house in Pacoima as he was getting ready to leave and join the others. He was charged with conspiracy, kidnapping, and false imprisonment, the same charges that were to be leveled against the other BSU members.

After hearing of Collins' arrest, the other BSU leaders called a meeting for the afternoon of November 6th at the Pacoima home of a black coed, Cornelius "Corky" Burroughs.

Art Jones recalls of that meeting:

"After Tim got busted, everything changed. When we met at Corky Burroughs' house, everybody was serious. I know how I felt before, and I honestly think others felt the same way, that the whole thing was fun and games. When we went to the Physical Education and Administration Buildings on November 4th, sure we wanted Markham fired, and when we changed from one to twelve demands,

67

we recognized that the demands were important—but I know I more or less got caught up in the excitement of the day, although if I could do it over again I wouldn't change anything I did.

"That day at Corky's after Tim got busted, it was no longer fun and games, we recognized the seriousness of what we were involved in. We knew that if Tim got busted, they were looking for us, and it scared many of us, because nobody felt we had committed a crime, and nobody felt like a criminal, but the fact still remained that the police were looking for us.

"There were two different groups going separate ways over at Corky's. There was the group I was in, which was mostly people who had been at the school for a few years, who I guess felt that maybe November 4th had gone too far. We wanted to go to the President and see if we could make a deal by promising him that we wouldn't push for the twelve demands, if the administration would drop the charges against us.

"Then there was Archie, and he is a rare leader. Archie had his group; it included Uwezo, Dancer, and others who were much more militant. We all respected Archie, for we knew he was not just a firebrand militant, although he could cut you to pieces with words, particularly with his large vocabulary. But we respected Archie because we had known him for a couple of years and we knew he was a serious and dedicated man, and that he put the interest of other people, of the group, over his own interests.

"It was mainly because of Archie that we decided to stick it out. It had never been fun and games to him. I don't want to sound like he was a serious, mean cat out to harm the administration, or all white people. Just the opposite. I remember when we were up on the fifth floor that day, one of the young brothers kept telling this white student not to come up. The crazy white boy was going to come up the stairs to the fifth floor anyway. So this young brother got a fire hose and was gonna wash the white boy down the steps before Archie stopped him and convinced the white boy he should go back. That day, time and time again, it would have gotten out of hand on the fifth floor if Archie hadn't had the respect of the brothers and sisters, particularly those young brothers.

"We all knew Archie was committed, and that day at Corky's he and his group argued that we should continue to press for demands, for they were important to black students who were already at, and who would be coming to the school. He also said that we shouldn't give in to the administration by saying that we were wrong, because we had used the only channels that were open to us, and there was nothing criminal about what we had done. The criminal act was the administration's lack of sensitivity to black students.

"Archie finally swayed us over. It was no longer fun and games. We decided we would stick to the demands, and go to jail if we had to, but we would not sacrifice our principles, what we had fought for. The possibility of going to jail drew us closer together and made us more committed."

They decided to get in contact with Legal Aid, an Office of Economic Opportunity (OEO) agency that supports indigent clients. Jack Diamond, a Legal Aid attorney in nearby Van Nuys, informed the BSU activists that the Van Nuys Superior Court had issued John and Jane Doe warrants for their arrests.

Diamond made an investigation and found out the names of the students who had been identified from the files—of the one hundred or more participants, twenty-seven activists (in addition to Collins) had been identified. At the request of the BSU he arranged for a group surrender to take place the next day before Judge James DiGuiseppe at the Van Nuys Superior Court.

Thursday, November 7th, at 11 A.M., Chatman and twenty-six other BSU activists went to Division 75 of the Van Nuys Superior court. The press and television were there for this arranged surrender. Judge DiGuiseppe in a short session arraigned the twenty-seven activists on a complaint that charged: *from October 29 to November 4, 1968, the defendants conspired to commit kidnapping, false imprisonment, burglary, and robbery* (the burglary and robbery were such outlandishly bogus charges that they were dropped almost immediately).

There were 74 charges against the twenty-seven Valley State activists—72 charges of conspiracy, kidnapping, and false imprisonment, and two extra charges of assault against Dancer. The bail ranged from $1,000 to $2,500 each.

After the arraignment, the students were shackled to each other by the foot and led out to a waiting bus in front of the courthouse. They were driven around the block to the Van Nuys City Jail, which is actually the back of the courthouse, and were locked up. For the next three hours they were questioned individually about what happened on November 4th.

That evening, Celes King, a prominent black bail bondsman and NAACP member, bailed them out. Within the next week, the local NAACP (with the support of their national committee) made a commitment to the imprisoned BSU students that they would follow their case through to the end.

The confrontation and demands had received national and local frontpage attention. Now the BSU settled down to the hard work of implementing its demands. Although, in accord with the Black Moratorium, black students were not attending classes, they came onto campus two or three times a week to hold rallies in the Open Forum in support of their demands.

Delmar T. Oviatt replaced Blomgren as Acting President of Valley State in December. After the rallies in the Open Forum, the black students and their supporters (usually totalling no more than 300 demonstrators) would march to the Administration Building and stand in front of the building chanting: "We want Oviatt!"

Oviatt never came down to address the demonstrators, and each time after going through the ritual of marching to the Administration Building and chanting for Oviatt, the students would disband peacefully. The ritual was always under close observation by fifteen to twenty police stationed daily in the equipment area to the side of the Administration Building. These men of the LAPD had been on duty at the school since the confrontation. (Chatman would say: "Look how much money we are costing Reagan.")

On Thursday, January 8, 1969 there was to be a major rally in the Open Forum. The Reverend James Hardgett of SCLC was to speak, as was Margaret Wright, a black woman leader from Los Angeles. Black community people from the Pacoima area, as well as a contingent from San Francisco State College, which at the time was also involved in a revolt, had been organized into motor caravans to come to the rally. There were also white ministers, civil rights activists, and student supporters.

This was to be *the* demonstration. It was well planned and organized, and there was general argreement that in deference to Reverend Hardgett, every effort would be made to keep it peaceful.

When demonstrators arrived at the Open Forum that morning, they saw police cars cruising around the site. They were warned by students and faculty that Oviatt had declared the campus in a "state of emergency," and that the police were on campus in full force. They decided that they would not be intimidated and continued with the rally.

It was an inspirational session. Hardgett blew. So did Chatman. And Margaret Wright, and the black student leaders from San Francisco State. Then the cry went up: "Let's go see Oviatt." The more than 400 demonstrators marched to the Administration Building.

The chant began: "We want Oviatt!"

The atmosphere was tense, for inside the Administration Building, in full view of the demonstrators, were more than fifty helmeted, billy-club-carrying police. Chatman, Hardgett, Burwell, Walker, and Wright decided to enter the Administration Building peacefully to see Oviatt. They were inside for about thirty minutes and their black constituency outside became restless. The rumor began to spread that "Maybe the pigs have ripped off our leaders."

The tension became too much, and a young black

student threw a planter through the front window of the Administration Building. It was on. The police came pouring through the front door, running past the white demonstrators, whacking at the blacks, male and female, with their billy clubs. The blacks could not get away from the police, for more than a thousand white students had gathered to see what was going on and had boxed them in.

In the melee that followed, many BSU members were seriously injured. Two of them, Sheldon Jones and Winston Freeman, almost lost eyes. Two hundred eighty-six people were arrested that afternoon; included were the five who had entered the Administration Building to see Oviatt (they were arrested for trespassing). But most important, that afternoon of violence showed that Valley State was on the brink of disaster unless the administration recognized the legitimacy of the BSU, and accepted their demands.

Late that afternoon Celes King bailed out the black students. (By nine the next morning, all 286 arrested for trespassing and interfering with school business had been released on $600 bail each.) A group of concerned white students from Valley State, in conjunction with an *ad hoc* committee of white ministers and civil rights activists, interceded with Acting President Oviatt on behalf of the BSU, although the BSU had not requested them to do so. A meeting was arranged to be held in Pacoima, late that evening, January 8th.

It became an all-night affair. Acting President Oviatt and several members of the faculty and administration were there. So were Chatman, Burwell, Uwezo, and Bostic for the BSU. The SDS was represented, and the Los Angeles City government sent Herb Carter, head of its

73

Human Relations Commission. The meeting worked out a series of compromises to halt Valley State's headlong rush toward disaster:

1. Cancellation the next day of the state of emergency imposed by Oviatt on campus that afternoon. The order had banned unauthorized campus meetings and prohibited non-students from coming on campus without special permission.

2. Return of the campus to regular operation with a ban on illegal, violent actions.

3. Resumption of Open Forum meetings that had been scheduled prior to the imposition of the state of emergency edict.

4. Representatives of various student organizations to be permitted to make presentations in classrooms with the permission of the instructor.

5. Police not to be called on campus.

6. The Acting President (Oviatt) to establish an advisory group to discuss the expansion of the school's black studies program and Mexican-American studies.

The next morning, January 9th, at ten o'clock, Chatman and the BSU held a rally at the Open Forum before more than 2000 people to explain the compromises and express the good will of the black students. There were no police in view, and it was a peaceful rally. More than a dozen speakers were on the platform, and Chatman, the keynote speaker, closed the three-hour rally by saying:

"I want you all to form up in a column and we're going to march across campus [to the Administration Building]. It must be quiet and orderly. We want to show the

Administration that we are reasonable people and that our requests are reasonable."

The students formed in a column six to eight abreast and moved quietly to the Administration Building four hundred yards away. On the steps of the Administration Building Chatman told the crowd: "I ask all of you to hold up your hands to give Dr. Oviatt a symbolic sign of your unity; to show him that we all want the same thing—meaningful change at this college."

The students all raised their hands and, after a few more minutes of demonstration, disbanded. That afternoon, Chatman and a few other BSU members, along with people from the black community of Pacoima, met for four hours with Dr. Oviatt and members of the faculty and administration. Out of that meeting came an advisory committee to expand Afro-American and Mexican-American Studies.

On June 3, 1969, Van Nuys Municipal Judge Irwin J. Nebron passed sentence on Chatman for failing to disperse during the January 8th rally. Judge Nebron fined Chatman $300, put him on three-year probation, *and ordered him to write a composition of not less than 5000 words on Civil Disobedience.*

During that month of June, 1969, the administration at Valley State relented—they recognized the legitimacy of what had become the major demand of the November 4th confrontation: the establishment of a Black Studies Department. The department was to be staffed completely by black men and women.

To interview applicants for positions on the faculty,

the BSU formed a committee made up of ten students who obtained the approval of the body of the BSU at a mass meeting before they submitted their recommendations to the faculty personnel committee. (Black Studies, or Afro-American Studies as it is called now, exercises a great degree of autonomy in hiring its personnel. There are two professors with tenure, John Bland and Hubert Palmer, on the faculty personnel committee. They were among the first hired in June 1969 for the new department and were immediately placed on the committee. There they maintained a strong influence in assuring that the remainder of the recommendations by the BSU faculty hiring committee would be followed.)

The sixteen faculty positions were filled that month. Ten black men and six black women were selected. The criteria used by the BSU's hiring committee were largely pragmatic—experience in the academic world was secondary to the ability to relate in a positive manner both to the black experience and to the subject matter they would be teaching.

Maxine Willis, a twenty-four-year-old ex-Chicago black community social worker with a Bachelor of Arts degree in social work who now teaches a course in Afro-American Studies, "The Black Family," talked about her interview with the BSU committee: "They questioned me about my academic credentials in social work, but they were more thorough in questioning me about my experience as a social worker in Chicago's black communities. I remember that I once used the word "ghetto," and a young woman on the committee objected, saying that the word was of Jewish derivation, and had a derogatory connotation when used in reference to black people in this country; and that black community was the proper expression. I had to agree with her, and I was impressed with this young woman's awareness. She couldn't have been more than twenty. I'm sure I was hired because I clearly expressed how the welfare system was negative for black people, how it created a class that was wholly dependent on white society, and that this class was powerless because of this dependency. I gave an example of how certain states might soon be experimenting with giving black mothers birth control pills with their welfare checks, using black mothers as guinea pigs in their genocidal experiments to keep the black population in this country at a controllable level."

Of the sixteen faculty members hired, all had B.A. degrees except for William Marshall, the drama instructor, a noted Shakespearian actor with years of experience in film and on stage, especially in black community theaters. Three of the faculty were working on their Ph.D.'s: Barbara Rhodes, Hubert Palmer, and John Bland. Tiyo Soga, who was to become chairman of the department, a black South African in exile who refers to himself as a "Pan-Africanist," already had his Ph.D. And the eleven other members include ex-BSU leaders Burwell (who became co-chairman of the department) and Walker; both were working on graduate degrees.

Only one recommendation of the BSU hiring committee was not accepted. It was the first recommendation made to the faculty personnel committee: that Archie Chatman be chairman of Afro-American Studies (née the Black Studies Department). Chatman was academically qualified in that he had graduated with honors that June with a

B.A. in history. Furthermore, the BSU hiring committee, with the unanimous support of the BSU body, was behind his nomination. The faculty personnel committee, with administration backing, rejected the nomination of Chatman for chairman of the department on the grounds that he was "unfit" because of his felony indictments and because of the possibility of convictions.

The BSU was ready to take the position, "No Chatman, no Department," their support of Chatman stemming from their recognition of the fact that his commitment had been the inspiration that had fired their activism and made Black Studies a reality.

"Archie had been the leader," BSU officer Rosalyn Emory recalls. "He had set the example. It was he who went to the meetings and confronted the faculty to get the EOP. He was the tireless worker always running around the campus rapping to the new black students about being black aware, and also to the older black students about making the Black Student Union stronger.

"Black people put their trust in a leader—a man who stands up. Someone who is willing and has the courage to express their feelings about their situation. That is what Malcolm was about. That's what Archie was about. He had been expressing our feelings about the situation at Valley State in his words and actions long before November 4th, and naturally he gave us strength and inspiration during the confrontation.

"He was the logical choice for chairman. We knew he was intelligent and creative enough to do the job, and there was no question about his commitment. The administration said he was unfit. Obviously they only looked upon him as an agitator, and as the ringleader of November 4th. We were determined there would be no department if no Chatman. But Archie convinced us that it was more important that we have a department than that he be chairman. He said he would work just as hard to make the department effective not being chairman, and that titles weren't important to him. He is an unselfish person, particularly when it comes to the struggle of black people."

Chatman cleared the only stumbling block between the BSU and the administration in the staffing of the Black Studies Department by turning down the nomination for chairman. Instead he worked that summer as an assistant instructor in college preparatory courses for incoming EOP freshman, under a grant from the Los Angeles anti-poverty Agency (EYOA), in addition to organizing with the BSU.

Now completely staffed, and retaining a chairman and co-chairman, the Black Studies Department began to work out a curriculum for the fall of 1969. Educational Resources Institute, a consulting agency based in St. Louis, Missouri, and Washington, D. C., which had experience in the area of Black Studies at major Euro-American-oriented universities and colleges, was hired to make recommendations on curriculum and the content of each subject in the curriculum.

Faculty members met three or four times a week during the summer months in an effort to become a tighter-working unit and to develop a curriculum for the department from the recommendations of the ERI and ideas of their own. (Also during that summer, the BSU began to have daily lunches at their new Black House with the faculty. They served to draw the faculty and the BSU student activists closer socially, and by charging a certain amount per plate also raised money for the BSU projects and bail bonds.)

From its inception in the fall of '67, the Valley State BSU had worked from the premise that they should organize first in the black community closest to that campus —which was Pacoima. They reasoned that work in the community was more relevant and of more immediate importance to black people in America than work on the Northridge campus. In a larger sense, it was a recognition that being at Valley State did not make them part of a Euro-American reality; that their roots were still entrenched in an oppressed, exploited segment of American society—black people.

Therefore, when the Valley State activists began to organize in the Pacoima community in the fall of '67, they were in effect following the same premise and rationale that the young black college activists of the non-violent movement in the South had operated under in the early '60s: *that the role of the black college student in America is to organize and raise the consciousness of the black community; to be the vanguard for revolution.*

In '67–'68 the emphasis shifted among black college activists. There was a high degree of politicization among black people, particularly black college students, in the wake of the cry for Black Power. The tactic became to seize and/or organize an economic-political-cultural power base wherever you were; at Valley State (and numerous other colleges and universities in '67–'68) this meant activism on campus until a department controlled by, and relevant to, black students was established. In a sense, this was an extension of black revolutionary ideology and tactics in the '60s, to recognize and deal with the inherent institutional racism in America, which is the bulwark of the Euro-American lifestyle.

Black activists at Valley State and on other campuses around the country (CCNY, Wisconsin, Cornell, etc.) clearly saw that institutional racism in this country would never be completely eradicated—for the only avenue by which a race of people may survive as an economic-political-cultural entity is by reinforcing the way they see things, their approach to life, through their institutions. On the other hand, these young black college activists realized through their experiences that the Euro-American approach had always been disadvantageous and was quickly turning genocidal for African people in America. Therefore, alternative institutions that would ensure their survival (in America) had to be established.

The Afro-American Studies Department at Valley State was such an alternative institution. To reach its full effectiveness it would have to become involved, enmeshed, in the black community, for, as the activists from Valley State realized, the survival of African people in America could not be determined individually; it would have to be done collectively.

It was this acceptance of the collective nature of the struggle for survival that led Chatman and the other BSU activists to again pick the community of Pacoima as the main object of their organizing. This was in the summer of '69 (at the time trial motions for dismissal of the November 4th case were still being heard), and unlike their first efforts in the fall '67, the BSU now were effectively programmatic.

Said BSU activist Howard Johnson: "We gained invaluable experience because of November 4th. And then there was the moratorium, and rallies, and pushing demands, and of course the trial. I know we all became much more committed, and when we went into the community that summer of '69, everybody knew what it was about. We knew that to make our commitment to black people relevant we had to work on programs that affect the day-to-day existence of people in the community. We had to take our commitment from the ivy-tower world of academe to the grass roots, where it really counts. That's where we come from, and where our sisters, brothers, mothers and fathers still are."

One of the most successful programs started that summer by Chatman and the other activists was for the young black children of Pacoima. The BSU was given the use of a church in the community, and every Saturday they would have a free lunch for a couple of hundred children from Pacoima.

"When people talk about violence of America," said Robert Uwezo Lewis, "they refer to what happened at My Lai in an international context, or what happened to Fred Hampton and the other Black Panthers in Chicago in a national context, or in the local communities they refer to the day-to-day examples of police brutality to black men and women. That is violence, but that is not the only form of violence happening to black people. There are more insidious, calculated forms of violence. One of the most insidious forms of violence perpetrated upon black people in this country is when thousands, possibly millions, of young black children—and that goes for other minorities also—are allowed to go starving, or to go underfed, for days without a hot meal, and in the richest country in the world. A country which makes farmers rich men by giving them subsidies, paying them not to raise food. That is why we had to go into Pacoima and try to help feed our people, because we knew America was willing to let them starve."

In addition to the free hot lunches at the Saturday afternoon nursing program, the BSU activists took the young black children on trips, and held classes for them. The trips were to places in Los Angeles, outside of their small community, such as parks, museums, etc. The classes were of two kinds: those that introduced the young black children to black history and culture, and those that improved their skills in reading and math.

That summer of '69 the BSU also started a program whereby they would canvass the grocery stores in the community and collect food. Each week they would make up a list of twenty to thirty families in Pacoima in need of groceries, and after canvassing the stores they would distribute the produce collected among the families. It was not restricted to black families—Mexican-American and poor white families that were in need were also included.

A progam of politicizing the Pacoima black community with leaflets door-to-door, and on the street corners, was put into operation. Some leaflets were purely informational, letting the community know of a cultural or social event to be given by the Black Student Union (or some other important black cultural or political organization in or around L.A.); some offered an invitation to attend one of the classes being given by the BSU; others were political propaganda addressed to a current political or cultural event that was important in the context of the black movement in America.

There was also on-campus activity that summer. The administration at SF Valley State had given the BSU a large house located on a lot which had been part of a sizable area of land adjoining the college, originally purchased with an eye to future expansion of the Northridge campus. The BSU converted this house into combination living and working quarters, and called it the Afro-American Studies Center (to black students on campus it became known as the Black House). During the summer, and the following '69–'70 school year, this center was used for social and cultural functions, as the site for black political education classes for black students on campus, and as a place to conduct study groups for black students and discussion groups among faculty and black students on matters of concern to African people in America.

The installation of the Afro-American Studies Center was celebrated as a landmark political act. The Center was painted green on the outside, and the interior was done in black and red. Red, black, and green are the colors of what is symbolically known as the black flag of America (in the last two years this color symbolism has caught on, and many young black brothers and sisters all around the country have begun to wear buttons and hats of red, black, and green). The red is for the blood that African people have spilt while being exploited and oppressed by the white man; the green is for the land—Africa—from which they were taken, and which was stolen from our African brothers still on the continent—the land which all Africans must retake; the black is for black people— beautiful people.

The Trial

There is an intractable problem with trials that have political implications. The people whose job it is to make the judgment or bring in the verdict, jurist or juror, will almost certainly have formed a position, pro or con, as to the political issues of the case against the defendants.

Therefore, if a jurist, let's say, is on the other side of the political issue from the defendants (a safe assumption, for a jurist is at gut level a law and order man who does not base his decisions on the philosophical justifications for changing society), and if you have a public climate that is incensed by the political activities or positions of the defendants, it is highly probable that the jurist will step outside the bounds of legal restraint, and with the zeal of a crusader become a self-appointed guardian warding off evil political positions as a threat to society.

In the late '60s, as the revolutionary/radical political forces intensified their efforts to effect change in America, there was a rash of political trials. Many took place in California, where the political climate was such as to make the state almost a model of the open polarization of American society. The Administration of Governor Reagan was notoriously conservative, and backed by a mostly conservative populace incited by influential right-wing elements, he acted under a mandate to move harshly and directly against the active and vocal revolutionary-radical elements in the state.

In '67–'68 in California, the political trials centered around the Black Panther Party and student dissidents. Student revolt threw the college and university campuses in California into turmoil in '68, with San Francisco State College and San Fernando Valley State College being the most violent and politically significant.

Sensing the outrage and confusion of the conservative citizens who put him into office, Reagan brought strong forms of repression against student dissidents (along with the events surrounding the Chicago Democratic convention, it was a sign of the type of repression that was to become a national policy).

On December 20, 1968, the Los Angeles County Grand Jury indicted twenty-eight activists in the San Fernando Valley State revolt. By the time the trial began on September 19, 1969 (the delay was due to numerous motions for dismissal), charges against four of the indicted had been dropped, leaving twenty-four activists to stand trial. That opening day, the Los Angeles *Times* called it: "One of the most significant criminal trials in the State's history." It was the first mass prosecution in this country of campus activists on felony charges. Judge Mark Brandler presided over the trial.

Each of the twenty-four defendants was indicted on seventy-two counts. The breakdown was: one count of conspiracy, thirty-four of kidnapping, and thirty-seven of false imprisonment. Dancer had two additional counts of felonious assault. It made for a total of 1730 counts. To many people's surprise, the defense waived its right to a jury trial, believing it would have lengthened the trial at least two months and considerably increased court costs, for not only would they have had to select a jury, but the jury would have had to bring back a verdict on each count.

"I never did go for waiving our right to a jury trial," said one of the Valley State activists, Robert Uwezo Lewis. "I knew that it would be a political trial, and I was prepared to have it drag on for months—as long as possible —so that we could politicize as much of the black community as possible to support our position.

"Archie and Eddie believed as I did that the trial was a sham, a game. It was clear to us from the beginning that District Attorney Evelle Younger and Judge Mark Brandler were in on a conspiracy with Governor Ronald Reagan to make political gain at our expense. Judge Brandler was up for an appointment to the appellate court at the time. Younger is an opportunist. Two years after the trial he is still getting on our back. In his campaign for Attorney General for the State of California [Evelle Younger ran for the post in the '70 election, and won], his television campaign commercials talk about his integrity, and offer as an example the fact that he was the only District Attorney who convicted student protestors when he prosecuted the San Fernando Valley State activists on felony charges. He is saying to the racists, the conservatives of California, that he won't stand for any shit.

"At the beginning of our trial in September, 1969, our NAACP lawyers convinced the other defendants that we would get a fair trial. Our lawyers had met with the Judge on several occasions in his chambers, and they had stated as part of their legal position that they were going to have Brandler removed from the case. Brandler then told them how 'he couldn't conceive how there could be any conspiracy.' The basis for the case of the prosecution was that they had to prove a conspiracy, because the rest of their evidence was flimsy. Our lawyers also told us that Brandler had chastised the prosecution attorneys in their presence for trying to charge us with a conspiracy with such flimsy evidence. Brandler had been contesting with other judges for this case, which he knew would be politically important to his career, and he was shrewd. By his statements in his chambers, he convinced our lawyers that he would be unbiased, and I guess they felt that because he was Jewish he would be a liberal.

"Our lawyers convinced the majority of the students that Brandler would be understanding, and that it would be foolish to have a jury trial. I don't believe our lawyers sold out, I believe they were out-smarted, and as a result we were co-opted from the start.

"This co-option lasted throughout the trial. They wanted us to act like pseudo-Negroes, who weren't aware

90

of what we had done. Most of us on trial, being young and politically immature, were convinced by the NAACP lawyers that that was the way the case should be handled. Archie, Eddie, and myself knew different. We realized what we had done, why we had done it, and that to capitulate from our position would not only be dishonest and harmful to objectives on the campus, but fatal to our case. But we were definitely in the minority, and it went the way of our attorneys."

The defense attorneys for the Valley State activists were Loren Miller, Jr., his cousin Halvor T. Miller, Jr., and Morgan Moten, all from the Los Angeles NAACP legal defense fund (according to National Executive Secretary Roy Wilkins, the legal services donated by the NAACP cost them $50,000 to $100,000).

In their opening statements to Judge Brandler, the prosecuting attorneys made clear what they felt to be the significance of the case. Bugliosi said: "Your verdicts, based on the evidence, will reflect the community sentiment on whether colleges and universities should be run by administrators or by students, and more urgently, whether campus militants are above the law of this state or if, like you and I, even the Governor, they are subject to its laws." Kenner underscored Bugliosi's statement: "Campus disorder and turmoil is one of the most serious problems and crises which face this nation today."

Attorney Morgan Moten opened his defense of the Valley State activists with a statement on how he viewed the case: "It is highly significant that after November 4th [1968], most of their [BSU] demands were met." And continuing: "If you send them to jail, it will be the biggest discouragement ever for black students throughout the United States."

In their brief as to the legal argument they would present in the case, the defense attorneys had said they would seek to prove "that the action was spontaneous and the students only intended to seek a redress of legitimate grievances."

The prosecution's brief implied that they were not contending, and did not intend to prove, that each defendant actually kidnapped and falsely imprisoned every victim. They were proceeding on the theory that each defendant was criminally responsible for every kidnapping and false imprisonment because all the defendants were co-conspirators and were aiding and abetting each other in carrying out a joint criminal action.

As the trial went on, the actions of both sides underlined the nature of the case. The American Civil Liberties Union moved to have the case thrown out of court because the defendants were indicted by a Grand Jury instead of by *complaint and information* (generally, when the prosecutors lack evidence and/or want to expedite matters, they call a Grand Jury, rather than use the complaint and information method of bringing charges, which requires more substantial evidence), and that was a denial of their constitutional rights. The motion was denied. Judge Brandler entered into the dramatics. He ordered extra police and security measures (searching), maintaining he had learned from a reliable source that on the first day of the trial "two spectators were armed with guns."

The trial received wide coverage in the news media

over its two months' duration. The primary evidence upon which Judge Brandler returned the convictions at the end of the trial was the testimony of witnesses.

It is important to note that the evidence was flagrantly contradictory. An example was two faculty members clashing over what happened in Arnett's office. Winningham said that Dancer put a razor against Arnett's neck and said: "If the man [police] comes in, you'll be the first to go." (It was this evidence that substantiated Judge Brandler's verdict of felonious assault against Eddie Dancer.) Charnofsky was also in Arnett's office (most of the time there were only three faculty members in Arnett's office, along with three BSU members), only one foot away from Winningham, and in his testimony he said, "I didn't see Dancer with a razor against Arnett's neck, and I never heard him make that threat." Charnofsky also contradicted Arnett's testimony by saying that he never saw him being jerked from a chair.

Former Acting President Blomgren also testified that although he signed a twelve-point agreement under duress, he did not consider himself to be either kidnapped or falsely imprisoned. And the BSU activists denied to a person any attempt at conspiracy, false imprisonment, or kidnapping. They wanted solely to present their grievance, their demand that Coach Markham be fired.

Dancer, who along with Chatman and Lewis was to receive the stiffest prison sentence, is highly articulate on the contradictory nature of the testimony, and the overall tenor of the trial: "The manner in which this trial was handled was ludicrous. There were countless incidents upon which a mistrial could have been based. In fact, our lawyers say that the state has absolutely no chance to have the convictions against us stand when the appellate courts hand down their decisions.

"In listing the overt irregularities of law that the prosecution committed and that the judge condoned, we can start from a few months before the opening of the trial on September 19, 1969. The District Attorney had given photos of us, the defendants, to his witnesses, two and three months before the opening of the trial. He gave his witnesses time to study the photos, and then called the witnesses into his office individually to go over the photos with them to make sure that they would be able to positively identify us when the trial started.

"Also, two or three months before the trial, he delivered to his witnesses individual copies of the Grand Jury transcript, our indictment. He was giving the state's witnesses plenty of time to study and memorize the Grand Jury transcripts, so that there would be no contradictions in their testimony at the trial and at the Grand Jury hearing.

"Under the examination at the trial, the state's witnesses confessed to having access to the photos and trial transcripts, and the Judge admitted that this was irregular, and admonished the prosecution. However, when our lawyers asked for a mistrial based on this, the Judge denied the motion.

"There were other flagrant procedural errors by the prosecution which should have been grounds for a mistrial. For example, when the trial started there were twenty-four of us. They had the defendants' seats numbered from one

94

to twenty-four. Each of us had a specific seat that we would sit in each session, for the duration of the trial. I had seat eight. The attorneys for the prosecution had told all of the witnesses which numbered seat each of us would be sitting in, so that they would be able to identify us.

"The identification of the witnesses was crucial to the case of the prosecution. With over one hundred people involved in November 4th, witnesses had to be able to identify positively, for the court record, the twenty-four of us, because the prosecution's case was based upon the fact that all of us had been beyond a doubt identified as participants, as conspirators.

"In spite of all the assistance, most of the time the witnesses were confused. Take Uwezo, for example. He had a long Afro on November 4th, but it was cut short by the time of the trial. The witnesses had a difficult time identifying him, so near the end of the trial the prosecution got permission from Brandler, over Uwezo's objection, to march Uwezo around the defendants' table, like a slave at an auction, in front of the Athletic Director Arnett. After Arnett got a good look at Uwezo, he got permission from Brandler to leave his the witness stand and go over to Uwezo and open his mouth, and look into it. Arnett then returned to his seat and positively identified Uwezo. I don't know, maybe he was identifying Uwezo by his breath.

"But even more important than the procedural miscarriages was the way the testimony was treated. Our testimony was disregarded completely, or frequently they would interpret similar testimony by us and the prosecution witnesses in a manner that was detrimental to us.

"Take for example the kicking incident between Dr. Spencer and myself. Dr. Spencer testified that I acted in a hostile manner toward him in his office on that day, and the essence of his testimony was that my hostility ended with me kicking him in the chest. I testified that I was talking to Dr. Spencer that afternoon about the kicking of the black football player by Coach Markham, and I asked him several times if he didn't think that the Coach's conduct was uncalled for. He responded each time that he saw nothing wrong with the Coach's conduct. I told him 'How would you like someone to kick your son,' and then extended my leg to his shoulder, and slightly pushed him, not kicked him, to demonstrate my point. The court obviously believed Dr. Spencer's testimony, for they found hostility in my act and convicted me of felonious assault because of the incident."

On November 18, 1969, Judge Mark Brandler found nineteen of the black activists from San Fernando Valley State College guilty of 588 counts of conspiracy, kidnapping, and false imprisonment (five students were acquitted for various reasons). The sentencing was set for January 28, 1970.

Before the sentencing, the Los Angeles Probation Department assigned a team to interview the defendants and file a report with Judge Brandler. The team consisted of Herbert L. Jones, H. Franklin Kissane, Fred Eisman, Clifford Clark, and Mrs. Margaret Boon.

In its report to Judge Brandler, the team recommended that sixteen of the students be released on probation and fined, and that the three others—Chatman, Uwezo and Dancer—have pre-sentencing psychiatric examinations. The team described Chatman as: "An affable, articulate man of twenty-two." It said of Uwezo: "He is bright and articulate."

At the sentencing, Brandler disregarded the recommendations of the probation department, and used personal reasons to justify the sentences he passed down. He referred in court to a meeting held at the Valley State campus after the convictions when Chatman allegedly (Brandler wasn't there) called him a "murderer." At the same meeting, Lewis allegedly referred to him as "a senile, decrepit 90 B.C. judge"; and Sheldon Jones was reported to have said he was a "fascist pig . . . lackey for Reagan."

Judge Brandler imposed on the nineteen students the stiffest sentences for campus activism in the history of America: Arthur J. Jones, $250 fine, and five years probation; Arrentia Holloway, $150 fine, and three years probation; Lidwina Apo, two years probation; Robert Dyer, three months in the County Jail, five years probation; Marion Kindle, two years probation; Michael Wrice, five years probation, three months in the County Jail; Jethro Collins, ten months in the County Jail, five years probation; Yvonne Robinson, three months in the County Jail, three years probation; George Brady, six months in the County Jail, five years probation; Howard Johnson, $250 fine, five years probation; Benjamin Caravo, three years probation; Vaya Crockett, six months in the County Jail, five years probation; Deardis Davis, $250 fine, five years probation; Arnold Boyd, five years probation; Sheldon Jones, one year in the County Jail, five years probation; Sharon Emory, three months in the County Jail, and three years probation.

Brandler said that he was fitting the sentences according to the degree of participation in the revolt. He judged that Archie Chatman, Robert Uwezo Lewis, and Eddie Dancer were the ringleaders, and sentenced each of them to one to twenty-five years in the state prison system, the most severe individual penalty ever given a campus activist.

In his statement to the defendants after sentencing, Brandler said: "College campuses are not privileged sanctuaries where disruptive, violent, felonious acts go unpunished." It was clear that he felt he had accomplished his mission. And Deputy Attorney Bugliosi echoed that assessment with probably the most succinct statement of the significance of the trial to conservative forces: "I would expect that militants all over the country were watching the results of this trial . . . it [the trial and verdicts] could have a crippling effect on campus militancy in this state, if not throughout the United States."

The harshness of Brandler's decision caught the black Valley State activists off guard, although it did not shock them. Most of them had understood from the beginning of the trial that the decision would be against them, for not only were they student dissidents, but, more important, they were black, and therefore Brandler, the judicial agent of the conservative forces, would view them in the total political context of the black man's struggle for liberation in this country.

Robert Uwezo Lewis told me: "Although we all felt from the beginning that we would be convicted, because it was necessary for Reagan and the other fascists in power in California to set the correct example for their followers, we never thought for a moment that our sentences would be as severe as they were. Not that we felt that Brandler and the state would be fair, for even the most naïve of us received invaluable political educations during the trial on the racism inherent in the American court system, but we never felt they would have the audacity, or be so foolish, as to come down on us as hard as they did.

"In my case, the Judge admitted to me before the sentencing that they had very little substantial evidence on me, because it had been difficult to identify me as being in Room 509 on November 4th. My Afro had been cut by the time of the trial. But he said he had to give me a harsh sentence because of my militant image. He was talking about my revolutionary rhetoric on television, in speeches and newspapers, concerning November 4th, and particularly in an April 1969 *Life* magazine feature on the revolt at Valley State.

"When I went to prison to serve my sentence, the Judge sent a copy of that *Life* magazine article as a part of my file to the prison authorities. He was making a superbad nigger out of me. A man to be watched."

In a campus speech he had made shortly before the sentencing, Uwezo stated: "The white man in this country has killed black people, and he has incarcerated black people, but that will never stop our legitimate fight for liberation."

It was clear to Uwezo that the conservative powers at the seat of government, who most clearly assume and guard the American cultural-political-economic hegemony of whites over blacks (and other non-whites) would be uncompromising with the black Valley State activists because they viewed their revolt as part and parcel of the black liberation movement in America, a movement that threatened the survival of America as a racist, exploitive, degenerate world power. It was also clear to Uwezo—and this feeling was shared by the others of the Valley State 19 —that this repression would not compromise their struggle —because that struggle was one of essential survival. It was because of this understanding—the need to survive culturally and politically in the hostile San Fernando Valley State environment—that November 4th occurred.

Uwezo said that neither incarceration nor death would stop the black movement for liberation. He was correct. What the trial and verdicts in the case of the Valley State 19 did was to reinforce the cultural-political awareness of black people. They saw clearly that these young black students, trying legitimately to survive, culturally and politically, at Valley State, received stiffer penalties than any of their white counterparts arcoss the country, and from this they saw that America was not willing (and I doubt will ever be willing) to allow the black man to exist with cultural or political freedom in her midst.

Afro-American Studies

During the fall of '69, eight of the twelve demands presented by the BSU students on November 4th were partially or fully implemented by the Valley State administration (the United Mexican-Americans were included equally in the implementation of the demands): a Black Studies Department leading to a B.A. degree; recruitment of five hundred black students per year until the racial population of the college became consistent with the national racial averages; tutorial facilities to be operated by the BSU to aid EOP students; investigations of employment practices on campus; a Black Faculty for the Black Studies Department (with a board half composed of black students to choose the faculty); disarming of the campus police; a grievance board to which black students could

101

bring complaints against faculty members; and weekly meetings with the President to make sure the demands and subsequent grievances would meet prompt and maximum college support. (The power to implement the most important of the other four demands—amnesty to the activists—was vested in the state, not the college.)

The population of black students at the Northridge campus doubled that fall, to three hundred. One hundred fifty black freshman EOP students were admitted. (In 1970 the total was over seven hundred.)

The Black Student Union got its department, and made the first important political departure from its November 4th objectives by changing the name of the new department from Black Studies to Afro-American Studies—and its own name to the Afro-American Student Union. The decision was arrived at after much discussion, its rationale being that "black studies" was not a positive identification for the program, that "Afro-American studies" more clearly addressed itself to the basic premise of developing the concept of Afro-American nationhood on campus.

This meant that the faculty of the Afro-American Studies Department would teach their courses from the perspective of the Africans' experience in America. The Afro-American Student Union realized that there was a rich and varied body of materials on cultural, political, and economic thought developed by the African since he was brought to this country in slavery; and that this body of thought, because it dealt with their reality, was more important to the black students on the Northridge campus than the European-white dominated education they would ordinarily receive.

It was the only realistic direction that the Afro-American Student Union could take. Individually and collectively they realized from the alienation they felt and the hostility shown them at Valley State, as well as off campus, that a black man's survival in this country hinged upon whether he could express in action the concept that his political, cultural, and economic ambitions were distinctly different from white America's (and therefore a threat to her) and were patently the same as every other black person's. And when a group of people have generally the same collective political, cultural, and economic ambitions, they aspire by definition to nationhood.

Therefore, the final objective of the Afro-American Studies program was to train black students to be able to go out into the larger black community beyond the Northridge campus and make the concept of Afro-American nationhood a reality; to build political and economic institutions in the black community that addressed themselves to black survival, while developing a great awareness of black culture.

An Afro-American Studies Department faculty member, Maxine Willis, talked of the beginnings of the program: "I know that I and other faculty members felt a sense of urgency when we started the program in the fall of '69. The students had made a tremendous sacrifice to get the department, and then we had it, and in a few months we had to develop our curriculum, reading lists, set up our major requirements. It was a tremendous responsibility, but we had some capable people and everybody was deeply committed and worked as a team.

"We worked very hard, and we were able to put together a comprehensive, integrated body of interdisciplinary courses—one we knew would provide black students with a meaningful educational experience because it prepared them to understand the past and present, from a realistic perspective. As aware as black people are today, particularly the young, you can't teach them history as if their ancestors came over on the Mayflower instead of a slave ship. We also knew that we had to teach the positive aspects of the black experience because of the historical unwillingness of the American educational system to accept and teach it, at the risk of destroying the myth of Anglo-Saxon superiority."

When Afro-American Studies began operations in the fall of '69, a South African, Dr. Tiyo Soga, took the reins as Chairman of the Department. Bill Burwell, the former BSU co-chairman, was appointed co-chairman of the Department.

There were sixteen black men and women (including the chairman and co-chairman) on the staff of Afro-American Studies in '69–'70. In keeping with a policy formulated by the Afro-American Student Union committee which, along with a faculty committee appointed by the President of the college, was selecting the faculty for Afro-American Studies, former Valley State activists who could qualify were appointed instructors in the Department. Included in these ranks was Jerome Walker, who had graduated with a B.A. in sociology in June, 1969.

A black student could take a major in Afro-American

Studies (or take a few courses, which counted as credit and fulfilled requirements, while majoring in some other department) toward a Bachelor of Arts degree. The major could cover a wide range of courses, but was also set up so that the student would have a minor in his field of expertise, i.e., Black Literature, Black Philosophy, etc.

The following are the requirements (with the number of credits noted in parentheses) for a B.A. degree in Afro-American Studies from San Fernando Valley State College as described in the department prospectus:

Lower Division

Core requirements 20 units, chosen from:

Geography and Culture of Pan African People (6) (Geography and Anthropology Division)

An analysis of Pan African cultural geography and a study of human behavior in Pan African Societies. A comparative study of Pan African cultural norms and their adaptations by the Afro-American to the U.S. culture. The emphasis is on features important to the understanding of current Afro-American problems.

Main Ideas and Issues in Black Philosophical Thought (3)

Analysis and discussion of the nature and the function of philosophy to the concrete needs of the Afro-American population. Based upon selected readings of traditional western philosophical thinkers and readings of current Black survival philosophies. A comparative study of the two, their relationships and their relevance.

EARL ANTHONY

Historical and Political Experience of the Afro-American (6)

A discussion of the development of the political structure and social institutions of the United States relating the politico-social dynamics to the experience of the Afro-American peoples, using the historical and political science perspectives as a frame of reference. Concentrates on the political-social development in the U.S. from Reconstruction to present times.

The Black Family (3)
(Sociology Division)

An analysis of the Afro-American family structure. Discussion of the sociological pressures and adaptation by the Black Family to those pressures. An emphasis on the roles of the Afro-American male and female in the family situation, and solutions to current negative sociological manifestations seen in the black family.

Economics of the Black Community (3)
(Economics and Math Division)

The study of Afro-American economic needs and their relationship to the overall organization of the American economy. Emphasis on the foundations of mathematical thought and its impact and usefulness in solving Afro-American economic crises. Practical math problems, fundamental geometry and algebra included in course work.

Afro-American Psychic Phenomena (3)
(Psychology Division)

The study of the psychological manifestations of oppression in the Afro-American. Emphasis on the understanding and analysis of psychological stress, the assessment of this phenomenon with discussion of solutions for the creation of a positive self-concept in Afro-American peoples.

Upper Division

Core requirements 20 units, chosen from:

Dynamics of the Afro-American Community (6)

An in-depth study of the contemporary state of the Afro-American community. The psyche of the black community, its economic, educational, and political features. Emphasis on isolating problem areas, and formulating plans for solutions. A basic requirement for all options in Afro-American Studies.

Interpretation of the African Experience I (3)

History and analysis designed to develop the student's interpretative understanding of the historical and political developments in African Societies. Concentrates on the peopling and foundations of African civilizations. Discusses pre-historical Africa to 700 A.D.

Interpretation of the African Experience II (3)

History and analysis designed to develop the student's interpretative understanding of the historical and political developments in African Societies. Discusses Africa from 1800 to the present.

Psychological and Sociological Foundations for Afro-American Education (8)

An introduction to the social, psychological, and philosophical foundations of education: their relation-

107

ship to the problems of American educational proc-
esses, and research into creating relevant teaching
standards and techniques for dealing with the Afro-
American. Requires 30 hours of field activities in
educational institutions within the black community,
also an in-depth research paper.

Electives Chosen from Below (9)

Religions in the Pan African World (3)
Great Men of Color I (3)
Great Men of Color II (3)
African People in the Third World (3)
Black Art (3)
Black Theater (3)
Derivation of Afro-American Music (3)
Selected Topics (3)

Barbara Rhodes, a professor of Black Literature in
the Afro-American Studies Department, commented on
the overall program: "Afro-American Studies is not remedial, or pre-college, nor does it represent a limited
version of general studies, although the courses are interdisciplinary. The Department is ethnocentrically geared
to the preparation of individuals trained to function in
black communities. And that can be the black communities
of black Africa, the West Indies, Latin America, and of
course, the black communities of the United States."

As to the curriculum itself, Mrs. Rhodes said: "We
used a five-point criterion in designating the curriculum
content: 1. relevance and importance of the topic to Afro-
American culture; 2. availability of the topic to an interdisciplinary approach; 3. sufficient value to merit inclusion
as part of the student's general education; 4. appropriate-

ness to lecture-seminar format with a heavy concentration on oral and written assignments; and 5. relevance to the student's interest and environment and appeal to his curiosity."

In its first year of operation, Afro-American Studies had no major problems, although there were the usual growing pains. The faculty of the department feel strongly that in the second year, '70–'71, they will improve on their performance, for they have a year of experience in which they gained familiarity and expertise in handling the curriculum and other responsibilities.

There are plans for expanding the scope of the department in the next few years. The black student enrollment doubled in '70–'71, from three to six hundred and it should continue to increase. Furthermore, it is hoped that there will be a full complement of sub-departments in standard disciplines: History, Natural Sciences, Physical Sciences, Political Science, Philosophy, English, Physical Development, Languages, etc.

Some of these sub-departments were in operation on a limited scale in '69–'70. As projected for future development, the Language Department would teach, along with English, languages that are part of the African experience: Swahili, Kikuyu, Arabic, French, etc. The Physical Development Department (equivalent of Physical Education) would instruct in Aikido, Karate, Thai Chi, Dance, The African Hunt, Gymnastics, Stick Fighting, Aquatics, etc.

It is clear from the first year's experience at Valley State that the concept of Afro-American Studies in white-dominated, white-oriented universities and colleges can revolutionize the educational process. It reverses a negative trend, for the universities and colleges have either been irrelevant, isolated institutions in dealing with the great problems which face this nation, or have capitulated to government, using their energies and talents to further America's downward course as a degenerate world power. Afro-American Studies can make a positive contribution, not only as a component of the college or university (or in high schools, and possibly grade schools), but also as an integral part of the black community of America (and the African world community): a vital force to bring about the nationhood so necessary for the survival of the African people in this country.

A people's most valuable resource is its human potential. The human potential of African people in America has been wasted over their years in this country primarily because of their oppression and exploitation. Whatever human potential has been developed, it has generally left the black community. The Afro-American Studies Department at Valley State is one case where that trend has been reversed. It has accomplished this reversal by working from the premise that what is relevant to African people in America today is their survival, a survival possible only when they realize that they have the same political, economic and cultural ambitions, that black students must be trained to understand this, and that the knowledge and skills acquired on campus should go toward making the concept of black nationhood a reality.

THREE

Where Do We
Go from Here?

The idea of writing this book came to me during the month of December '69. I had been talking to my sister, Barbara Rhodes, and her husband Russell, about the direction of Afro-American Studies. It was a subject each of us was keenly interested in. Barbara was an associate professor of Black Literature at Valley State, and Russell was the Administrative head of Minority Studies (which included Afro-American Studies, Mexican-American Studies, and the EOP) at the University of California at Los Angeles. My interest stemmed from the fact that Afro-American Studies was an integral component of the African's struggle for liberation in America, which related it to Pan-Africanism, a movement to which I was deeply committed.

As we talked that night in December, Barbara began

113

to fill me in on what had happened at Valley State, and why. I remembered the revolt, but I also remembered there had been many black student revolts since '66, and particularly in '68. What were the parallels between the events at Valley State and the black student revolts at Cornell, Wisconsin, and all the other campuses?

It became clear as we went on that they all had certain common goals. The primary one was to institute an Afro-American Studies Department, and the others followed from that: to achieve a sizable increase in the enrollment of black students at the college or university; to have the university or college recruit from the black community, making the academic requirements flexible where necessary; to recruit black faculty members to staff the Afro-American Studies Department; and to win recognition of the courses in the Afro-American Studies Department as interdisciplinary so that it was possible to major in and earn a degree in Afro-American Studies.

It occurred to me also that there were strong similarities in the ideology of the Afro-American Student Union movements on the different campuses around the country. The black students confined the thrust of their attack to the racism inherent in the Euro-American university system, a byproduct of the racism inherent in Euro-American society. And almost without exception, there were friction and ideological conflicts with their white counterparts on campus, organizations such as SDS, which were more concerned with national issues such as America's involvement in Southeast Asia. In white radical circles, this ambition of the Afro-American Student Unions to build an institution, an Afro-American Studies Department, inside the university was looked upon as reformist, whereas their objectives, to attack on the basis of national and international issues and tear down the university which was representative of what they were against, were considered revolutionary. Yet, black activists such as myself, and other aware African people in this country, realized that at gut level much of the energy expended by white radical students was youthful "adventurism," an extension of a psychedelic life style, and if the pressure got too great, or their ambitions remained frustrated, these white students could easily cut their hair, put on a tie, and flow back into the fringes of respectable Euro-American life style. On the other hand, black students realized that in fact their objectives were revolutionary, for they dealt with survival. And that meant building an institution which reinforced a survival ideology, and at the same time taught skills that would make the survival of an African people a reality.

At this point in the conversation, I said: "With all the similarities in objectives and ideological thrust in the Afro-American Student Union movements in this country, it is important that black people, particularly black students, understand those similarities."

"I think they do," Barbara said.

"I know they do, but it's still important that at all times we have a historical perspective of our struggle, so that we do not repeat our errors. Even though black students know the similarities in ideology and objectives, between, let's say, Cornell and Valley State, they still have to be documented."

And so I decided to write this book. I would use the

San Fernando Valley State College revolt as a model, for its objectives (an Afro-American Studies Department, etc.), ideology (racism as the major problem facing Africans in this country), and tactics (seizure of administrative buildings, etc.) were representative of all the various Afro-American student movements in the late '60s.

I went back to New York in early January. About three weeks later I received in the mail from Barbara (no accompanying note) a Pacoima community newspaper called *Black World*. On the front page was the headline: *1–25 Years for Taking Over a Building*.

My first reaction was "It could only happen in jive-ass, John-Birch California." Yet as I read on, I realized I had related emotionally, instead of politically, to the news. I knew better. I knew that America was moving quickly towards open facism, and that a scapegoat would be needed when she could no longer resolve her internal contradiction of racism hand-in-hand with economic exploitation. Black people have always been politically, culturally, and economically polarized from the Euro-American life style. And historically, America has exploited the man of color, within her boundaries and abroad. Her insane commitment to this destructive course has created a new polarization within her white ranks, a disenchanted minority among people of Euro-American origin.

As Euro-Americans began to fight among themselves (a perfect example being the violent clashes between the laborers, "hardhats," and the student protestors in New York in spring '70), the political powers, national and local, would have to have a scapegoat, so that Euro-American people could unify and move against a single, easily identifiable source of their troubles.

It was clear that the scapegoat would be black people, as it has always been in this country. And it was also clear to me, as I analyzed the Valley State situation, that it was only one—very harsh—example of the type of political repression that black people in this country will be subjected to in the '70s, as America moves toward open fascism. (Another was the semi-official persecution of the Black Panther Party, of which I had once been a member.)

At that moment I felt a sense of urgency in the Valley State story. I realized that Archie, Eddie, and Uwezo, as well as the other sixteen activists, were political prisoners, and that the political ideology and objectives for which they were sentenced to prison should be given exposure, so that people could judge whether they had been treated justly.

I contacted Barbara, and she told me of plans being made to raise funds to bail Chatman, Lewis, and Dancer out of jail when their case went to appeal. Around April she called me back. Chatman, Lewis, and Dancer had been bailed out. I asked her to arrange a series of meetings for me with the Valley State activists.

She did, and on June 7th I went to Los Angeles for the first meeting, set up at Barbara's house for ten o'clock that night.

Chatman was on time. With him was Ronnie Hill, a young black student who couldn't have been over eighteen, and Archie's brother Lewis, a tall, goateed black activist.

117

Barbara and the three Valley State activists were close friends, so the night started off in a comfortable social mood. I remember they talked about each other's children (Chatman's wife Linda was also sentenced for her part in the November 4th revolt; they had married on campus during that period of turmoil late in '68, and had recently had a child).

As the conversation switched from social to political matters, Lewis Chatman asked me "Why did you split from the Panthers?"

"I didn't believe politically in coalitions with white folks," I answered, "and I didn't believe ideologically that class is more important than race in the revolutionary struggle."

"I agree with that," said Archie, with his usual quiet and serious demeanor.

We had some common ground, and this served as the basis for the start of our talks; we went on to find other points upon which we could agree concerning the direction of the struggle of African people in America.

"What have you been doing since you left the Party?" Chatman asked.

"I've been reading and writing," I said, "mostly analyzing my experiences and becoming more sharply defined politically. What have you been doing since you got out of jail?"

"I've had to get a job. Uwezo and I are working for a brother out in Pacoima, cleaning out houses that have just been built. Have to support my family," Chatman said, measuring his words.

118

"Do you ever intend to continue your academic education?" I asked him.

"I do. I can't go back to Valley State, but I'm trying to go to UCLA, and it looks like I'll be accepted into their graduate program. I'll probably start around February '71."

"What about Uwezo and Dancer?"

"Uwezo is also applying for UCLA. I think he is going to be accepted and will also start in February 1971. Uwezo will be a junior and is talking about changing his major from liberal arts to chemistry, a technical skill that will be needed for building the black nation here and in Africa. Eddie, he's going to Africa this year, he wants to study there."

"How long did you, Uwezo, and Dancer spend in prison?" I asked Chatman.

"We were in for four months, and then were bailed out when the appeal on our case was granted. First they sent all three of us to Wayside Max. The 'Max' is for maximum security. It was that type of prison. Then we were sent together to Chino, and we were all put in the hole. They called us unknown quantities. After a month we were sent to Tracy, so that we could undergo diagnostic study. Parole officers from the California Adult Authority talked to us at length about the Valley State revolt, the reasons for our participation, that sort of thing. They recommended parole for us. Uwezo and I were paroled from Tracy. Eddie was sent up to Vaccaville for some further tests, and he was paroled from there."

(Dancer was to tell me later: "When I began serving

119

time for November 4th, one of the prisons they sent me to was Vaccaville. They sent me there because they said I had social adjustment problems, because I had kicked Dr. Harold Spencer [Vice President of Administrative Affairs at SF Valley State], and because I had told them I felt exploited because I had worked in the cotton fields of Texas when I was young. They said I needed psychotherapy. I kept telling them that the exploitation I felt from my youth in Texas is the same exploitation—only different in kind but not in degree—that most all blacks are subjected to in the cotton fields of the South, or the urban ghettoes of the North. But they couldn't relate to that.")

I carefully phrased my next question to Chatman. "When you had your revolt at Valley State in '68, other BSU's all across the country were also revolting, and San Francisco State in particular had been under siege for at least six months before November 4, 1968. Did this influence you?"

"Of course it did. I don't mean that we revolted because they were revolting, because it was something to do. Our revolt was a direct result of the objective conditions at Valley State, conditions we sought to change by our twelve demands. But we *were* caught up in the spirit of that time. The black students on campus were ready—like all other black people—and this spirit of being ready to take whatever means were necessary to change our plight was infectious. It spread from city to city, from campus to campus."

"Was there anything else?" I interjected.

"We moved around and visited other campuses and saw what the BSU's were doing. Is that what you mean?" Chatman asked.

"Right on!"

"Yeah, we visited San Francisco State and Cal Berkeley the semester before. They were more or less the vanguard."

"Did they support you after your revolt?"

"They did," Chatman said. "We were invited to all the campuses in the Los Angeles County area, by the black students, and we talked about the revolt, and particularly our demands. Delegations from the San Francisco State College BSU would come down regularly for our confrontations with the Administration after November 4th."

"Are you still organizing?" I asked.

"I'm still organizing," he answered immediately. "I can't go on Valley State's campus and work, that's one of the restrictions on my appeal bail bond, but I've been organizing in Pacoima, in the community. Uwezo, and some of the other brothers who were in November 4th, are also working in the community."

"What exactly are you doing in Pacoima?" I asked.

"It's a large black community out there, and they're pretty much together. I mean they stick together. More or less we just talk to brothers and sisters trying to give information and facts where we can. I guess you would say that we're involved in politicization in Pacoima."

"What do you think are your chances on appeal?" I asked.

"I don't know. Our lawyers think we have a good chance. It was clearly a political trial, and Brandler made a political decision. . . ."

"One time this prosecutor," Lewis Chatman interrupted, "told Uwezo to open his mouth. And he checked his teeth, just like that bullshit they did in slavery."

Ronnie Hill added, "Once that racist prosecutor got mad because a witness, who was up on the fifth floor that day, couldn't identify some of the defendants." Everybody laughed.

Archie became serious again. "I had always hoped since it was a political trial—and I think we all knew of us—that the trial and even our prison sentencing from the beginning that they would try to make examples would at least serve to unify the revolutionary black activists at Valley State, and in Pacoima."

"We can't afford that anymore," I said. "I know that happened with Huey Newton; but what essentially happens is we have a cause célèbre, a martyr to organize around, and once that is over, we are no longer unified. We've got to organize around ideology."

"I agree," said Chatman. "I was just facing the realistic situation that we were going to be sentenced to prison terms. But it's better that I'm out, because I know the real work is organizing the brothers and sisters in the community. That's what we're beginning to do now."

"So then most of the people involved in November 4th are still active?"

"Right," Chatman replied. "Some are working in the community, and some are still active trying to build Afro-American Studies."

Barbara added. "Most of the activists are in Afro-American Studies. Some who were involved at the beginning of the black movement at Valley State are in positions of responsibility. Like Bill Burwell, who is co-chairman of the department, and Jerome Walker."

"So there is a close working relation between faculty and your Afro-American Student Union movement."

"Very close," said Barbara. "Everybody is committed to making the department work, both students and faculty, and everybody is committed to the overall black struggle. I mean nobody can just come in and get a job, and make good money, and only worry about teaching their classes. It's more than a job. We have every faculty member contribute 10 per cent of his salary each month to a fund."

"A survival fund?" I asked.

"That's what it is. The money goes to pay bail when necessary, but the NAACP has covered most of that. So it's used mostly for political and cultural projects, like our newspaper, *Black World*."

"We put it out once a month," Ronnie Hill added. "Next year we're going to try to put it out more. I'm the editor, and our staff is from the Afro-American Student Union, but we circulate the newspaper in the Pacoima community."

"So you also begin to politicize black folks in Pacoima through your newspaper," I commented. "That's hip. The Muslims do that, and so do the Panthers. We need as much of that as possible."

"Right on!" said Lewis Chatman.

"How is Afro-American Studies doing?" I asked.

"We're having a faculty retreat this week," Barbara said. "I was in D.C. with a few other faculty members for the Pan African Conference in April. We heard Stokely Carmichael's tape on Pan Africanism, and we talked about it when we came back. We discussed accepting Pan Africanism as the ideological direction for our department."

"How would you make it functional?" I asked.

"If we accept Pan Africanism as our ideology, and as Stokely says 'look first to Africa,' then we would adjust our priorities. For example, I'm going to suggest to the faculty at the retreat that in the next couple of years we should adjust our priorities in recruitment of black students. So that in a few years, if we have one thousand black students we can recruit for Afro-American Studies, the Department can make it mandatory that seven hundred of those slots be alloted for black students in technical and scientific fields."

I tried to expand her point. "Therefore, you would move the department to a higher functional level of Pan-African nationhood. You could train black students to be able to build a highly technical society, and those skills could be used in Africa or America."

"Exactly."

The conversation then drifted into a discussion of Pan Africanism. I told them I was committed to that ideology, that I had recently talked to Stokely Carmichael and agreed with him that revolution is essentially about land, and that there is land in Africa to build revolutionary bases that will work toward the liberation of African people around the world.

Everybody in the room expressed a commitment to Pan Africanism, and they agreed when I said: "It will have as many black people in this country relating to it as the King movement did in the early '60s."

A Few Afterthoughts

The SF Valley State 19 (and this applies also to the black activists at CCNY, Wisconsin, San Francisco State, Cornell, etc.) did not step into a vacuum when they began their campus activism and militancy in '68. The way had been prepared for them by eight years of a black student movement whose activities were mostly off-campus, in Southern communities, and which was a driving force within the larger black liberation movement that had begun to gather force in the mid '50s.

When this black student movement began in '60, Chatman was thirteen, and most of the others of the Valley State 19 were younger. Raised in this climate of heightened black militancy, revolutionary rhetoric, and black cultural awareness, it is not surprising that by '68 they felt

127

the kind of urgency that led them to assume the role of activists, to contribute their part to the black liberation movement.

The black student movement turned its struggle in '68 to attacking the Euro-American college and university system, and it is important to note that the Afro-American Student Unions across the country recognized their struggle as a question of self-determination. Black people, in their view, would have to control the political, economic, and cultural institutions affecting their lives, among which educational institutions were paramount. The sit-in movement of the early '60s placed its emphasis on integration, rather than control, and this is perhaps the clearest difference in the development of political consciousness and black cultural awareness through the '60s.

The SF Valley State Afro-American Student Union revolt of November 4th was successful in that it forced the college administration to recognize the black students' right to self-determination, to institute an Afro-American Studies Department. Now, two years later, black students and faculty at Valley State have made that concept of self-determination a working reality.

As I have already pointed out, Afro-American Studies has worked basically from the premise that the department must develop the concept of Afro-American nationhood among black students on campus, and prepare them to teach that concept in the black community. This makes the department potentially revolutionary. African people in America have the same ambitions—political, cultural, and economic—and these are considered markedly different from those of the Euro-American people who dominate American life. The black faculty at Valley State has taken this concept of Afro-American nationhood to a more sophisticated level by making it mandatory that over 70 per cent of all students in Afro-American Studies major in technical or scientific disciplines. The assumption is that we have enough black people in the social services, and that technical and scientific skills are immediately necessary for building a modern technological society, whether in Africa itself or any other place African people live. This should quiet such critics as the civil rights liberal Bayard Rustin, who once said of Afro-American Studies: "What in the hell are soul courses worth in the real world? No one gives a damn if you've taken soul courses. They want to know if you can do mathematics and write a correct sentence."

Of course there were sacrifices that had to be made by some of the black activists who participated in the November 4th confrontation, by three men in particular— Archie Chatman, Eddie Dancer, and Robert Uwezo Lewis —who were singled out by Judge Brandler as the ringleaders and sentenced individually to one to twenty-five years. Their cases are still on appeal, but it was clear that Judge Brandler was making an extreme example of these three men to serve as a political signal to other student demonstrators of what they might expect. Defense attorney Morgan Moten spoke to the point when he stated that he "believed the sentences were stiff because the students were black." Again, the question had been raised whether a black man is morally or legally obligated to obey the laws of a country in which he realistically has no political voice with which to express his disagreements.

Although the Valley State activists, a small minority struggling for the right to exist politically and culturally in a hostile environment, were sentenced to prison terms, their demands to rectify the situation were, for the most part, implemented. And Chatman and the other activists have continued to work in the struggle for the liberation of black people, showing again that penalties do not deter men when their consciences are aroused.

For black students on Euro-American dominated university or college campuses, '68 was, in the words of the poet José Martí, "the time of the furnaces." Campus after campus was rocked by revolt—at San Francisco State, Cornell, Wisconsin, CCNY, and numerous others. Afro-American Studies were instituted on all those campuses, as well as at campuses which did not revolt but indirectly felt the pressure. Yet in the last two years black students have been relatively quiet across the country (the killing of two Jackson State students in May '70 has been the only major incident on campus involving black students). They have been in the process of consolidating their gains, of structuring and building institutions that will educate African people in America.

Many black faculty and black student activists now recognize that well-established Afro-American Studies, although important in many respects, is not the ultimate goal. As Archie Chatman said to me about the demands of the Valley State BSU: "We realized that these demands were reformist, and not revolutionary . . . but they addressed themselves to concrete issues the people could relate to. . . ." Chatman saw that leadership could take any one of three positions: with the people, behind the people, or ahead of the people. He realized that if they were behind the people they would be irrelevant, and if they were ahead of the people they would be isolated. So their activism was for an Afro-American Studies program, something that all black people could relate to at that time.

As we look to the future of Afro-American Studies (or African-American Studies as they will probably be called), we can make one important assumption: the polarization of ideological differences with the controlling Euro-American component of the American college and university system will continue, paralleling the same polarization occurring outside the campuses. This means that as African people in this country become more sharply self-defined, they will realize that Afro-American Studies is not in itself enough for the needs of nationhood, for it is still dependent on, if not controlled by, the Euro-American component which will always have an influence over Afro-American Studies even without actual control.

Therefore, as an ultimate goal, the answer clearly becomes the African University, located in the American communities where African people live, supported by those communities, and drawing its faculty from those communities. (Many of this faculty will have been trained in Afro-American Studies programs at Euro-American universities.) An African University will, to a large degree, give African people in America the means to develop the skills and learning which are necessary for nationhood, to make them self-sufficient. And self-sufficiency is *the* vital objective if African people in America are to be liberated.